Elizur Wright

Politics and Mysteries of Life Insurance

Elizur Wright

Politics and Mysteries of Life Insurance

ISBN/EAN: 9783337123673

Printed in Europe, USA, Canada, Australia, Japan

Cover: Foto ©Suzi / pixelio.de

More available books at **www.hansebooks.com**

POLITICS AND MYSTERIES

OF

LIFE INSURANCE

BY

ELIZUR WRIGHT.

BOSTON:

LEE AND SHEPARD, PUBLISHERS.

NEW YORK:

LEE, SHEPARD AND DILLINGHAM.

1873.

CONTENTS.

Contents.

THE POLITICS AND MYSTERIES

OF

LIFE INSURANCE.

Chapter I.

In the United States more than half a million of persons, chiefly men, have their lives insured for the benefit of those who will survive them, or, in many cases, for their own benefit, if they survive a designated age. The business is done entirely by corporations, more or less "mutual" in their constitution or charter, more or less regulated in their conduct by State laws, and more or less preyed upon by State officials.

These corporations, few of which are over thirty years old, differ exceedingly as to the extent and amount of their business, and the magnitude of their resources ; their number of policies ranging from less than one thousand to more than seventy thousand, and their assets, exclusive of future premiums, from less than $100,000 to more than $50,000,000. We have in fact the anomaly of a company, having an annual revenue of $15,000,000, with about $60,000,000 in hand, which though constitutionally "mutual" and theoretically perfectly democratic, is, *de facto*, autocratic, the chief officer holding proxies enough to secure his own reëlection, in spite of any opposition short of the miraculous. An autocracy may be the best government in the world or it may not be, according to the character of the autocrat. The prejudices of our country are certainly not in its favor. In the politics of life insurance, whenever this autocracy takes place, the individual constituent, or "mutual member," finds that if he would retreat from a position where he is a political cipher, he must make a sacrifice of money in some sort of proportion to the time he has occupied it. He perceives, rather to his dismay, that he went in without stipulating with due caution the terms on which he could get out, in case he should become dissatisfied. If he had exercised that prudence, the autocracy of the corporation would have been under heavy bonds for its good behavior, instead of holding the members under heavier and heavier bonds, to acquiesce in whatever it should please to do.

That the life-insurance policy, in its usual form, is not a bargain which both parties enter into with their eyes open to all its contingencies, is sufficiently obvious, from the rapid rate at which policies are cancelled, with more or less loss to the individual, and sometimes with a loss, though generally with a gain, to the company. The rate of cancellation has so much increased of late, that in many companies hardly half of those who enter having bargained to pay from ten to fifty annual premiums, should they live long enough, ever pay the second. A recent State Report, shows 150,000 policies terminated in a single year, and only about 139,000 new ones entered. The fact that under the ordinary form of policy, the longer one stays in the company, the more it costs him to get out, must have something to do in accounting for this immense outward scramble. It cannot be that all these people have backed out because they have ceased to need insurance, or have found themselves mistaken in supposing that they needed it. The supposition is more reasonable that they have discovered the bargain was not quite fit to be made, and that inasmuch as there is a considerable probability that the necessity for insurance will not continue through the term of the policy, it is better to cancel it while the cost is at its *minimum.* They may also have discovered that there is far more mystery than democracy in life insurance, no matter how purely mutual the plan. They may have discovered that a life policy under certain legal provisions, designed to protect the interest of the beneficiary, is equivalent to a man's making a will which he cannot himself annul. Few men with their eyes open, would do this, even if the law allowed it.

The object of this volume is to show that all the real benefits of life insurance can be obtained under a policy which can be perfectly understood by both parties, without obliging the individual to submit to any wrong at the hands of an autocratic or pseudo corporation, a policy which provides fairly and equitably for the contingencies of the party's ceasing to need insurance, or being unable to pay for it, as well as that of his death.

There are two ways of providing for a surviving family : 1. Insurance, pure and simple ; 2. Accumulation. The former is immediate. It creates an estate instantaneously—so far as the interest therein of heirs is concerned. The latter is slow, entirely too slow for the particular exigency, though it has the advantage that it will benefit the party himself in time. Yet it is what every man attempts, or ought to, whether he insures or not. Of insurance, pure and simple, when you cease to pay and still live, there is nothing left. It would be a somewhat improvident citizen who should insure his life as long as it continued to be productive, and surviving that period, should have to resort to the poorhouse for his own support.

For the purpose of insurance, life is divided into units of time, each measuring a year, during which the risk is assumed not to change, but from any one

year of age to that which succeeds it the risk in
creases according to an assumed scale, which is
founded on the mortality observed of a large number of lives of the same ages under similar circumstances. Insurance, pure and simple, is when the
risk of each year, no more and no less, is paid for
at the beginning, in the course of, or at the end of
the year. The perfection of it in theory is what is
called "coöperative insurance," where, for example,
a thousand persons agree to pay $1 each to the fam-
ily of each deceased member. If the agreement is
carried out, the first that dies, in consideration of
his own obligation to pay, having actually paid
nothing, leaves his family $999, drawn from other
members. The second leaves $998. And so on.
If the lives were *all of the same age*, and unexceptionable in health, an equal payment would be fair,
and the number of them within a year could be so
nearly predicted as to make it practicable to provide for the death-claims by paying in advance, that
is, by premiums equivalent to the risk of the year.
If such premiums only were paid, there would, if
the calculation proved correct, be nothing left at the
end of any year; and every year, as the vitality of
the party decreased, the premium for the year
would increase. This premium for a given sum
insured, increasing every year according to the
increased chance of the party dying in that year, it
is convenient to call the *natural premium*. Insur-

ance, pure and simple, would be by the payment, annually, of these natural premiums. But in reality it does not exist, for reasons that are too obvious to need statement. The "coöperative plan," so far as it illustrates pure insurance, may be set down as impracticable.

What does exist, is a plan which combines in the same policy a series of pure and simple *yearly insurances*, with a plan of *accumulation* by *annual* deposits. And these two processes are so undistinguishably blended in the policy, as to be a perfect mystery to the insured, if not to the officers of the company itself. The insured generally agrees to pay an equal annual premium, either during the whole term of the policy, or a considerable part of it. He knows pretty well that this is larger than the "natural premium," or what it will cost to insure the amount of his policy the first year. But he is not told in the policy how much of it is for the first year's risk, and how much for accumulation. All the information he can get is, that inasmuch as his policy covers many years, including those future ones in which it will cost more than the whole of his premium to insure the amount of his policy for one year, the company must have something to accumulate to supply the deficiency. He is thus persuaded to leave this matter of the accumulation entirely to the company, and is probably enticed into an agreement that in case he fails to pay any premium when due, he shall forfeit the entire accumulation in the company's hands, or when he wishes to surrender, shall have only what he does not value, a small "paid-up" policy.

Now what is quite plain is, that the policy which combines insurance with accumulation is the right practical thing, *if under the right conditions*, inasmuch as every person who needs insurance, also needs to accumulate, so that if he survives the proper period of insurance, he shall have the enjoyment of a more or less considerable accumulation, and because insurance pure and simple is really impracticable, for the want of a sufficient security for the persistence of the natural premiums.

The permanence of the company depends not only upon the premiums being adequate to the risks assumed, but upon the policy-holder's being sufficiently bound to continue, so that the company may have a broad enough basis to realize death-claims nearly according to the assumed law of mortality. Precisely what the penalty of a non-performance of the contract on the part of the policy-holder should be, may be a matter of some doubt or difference of opinion. But that, if possible, it should be greater at the end of the first year than ever after, is simply a *matter of demonstration.*

Here is a blunder more than a hundred years old. The penalty has been a constantly increasing one ! It makes a perfect farce of the *accumulative* feature of the policy. It, in fact, enlarges a salutary penalty into a system of betting or gambling on persistence, totally unnecessary and foreign to the aim of the business.

It has been the lot of the writer to be connected practically with life insurance for many years, either as an agent, a state commissioner of insurance, or an actuary. In the latter capacity he has had frequent occasion to ascertain, by various standards, the proper reserve which a company should have, to make distribution of surplus, and to give an opinion on the value of one company's business to be transferred to another. Commencing with a profound conviction of the usefulness of a policy to himself, and no knowledge of the principles of the business whatever, he assumed that science had done for it about all that it could, and for a long time took it for granted that what it had not done could not be worth doing. But old blunders will always show themselves when run into new fields. One, which, though very mischievous when confined to the ordinary whole-life policy—a policy which itself commits another blunder of covering years of life that are really uninsurable—, might have been tolerated or escaped observation a century longer, forced itself upon his attention when the American appetite for independence and *self-insurance* had multiplied endowment policies, of not very long terms. This sort of policy, which is the very

perfection of life insurance, the very thing for a
high-spirited young man to take, by applying to it
the old blunder that always adhered to the life policy of putting expenses and commissions as a percentage on the premium, was converted into a *swindle*. It was a swindle not easily detected, immensely profitable to the agent, but intensely unsatisfactory to the policy-holder after being found out.

The headlong rush into endowment policies,
which began about fifteen years ago, without correcting the British error in loading the premiums and
assessing expenses, and without distinguishing between the *insurance* and *self-insurance* of a policy,
is what has brought life insurance in this country to
its present grief. This volume is designed to call
public attention to the subject in such a way that
our companies, which, in spite of all their errors,
are generally in a sound condition, shall be obliged
in their future business to give endowment policies
that are fit to be made. When this is done, there
will be small demand for any other kind.

The first thing to be done is to achieve a distinct
definition of the terms we shall have occasion to use.

SELF-INSURANCE.

This element of a life-insurance policy always
exists whenever more than the natural premium for
a single year, with the working expenses thereof,
is paid. It is the same as the *reserve* on the policy,

1*

at the end of the year, and is commonly called the
value of the policy. The propriety and significance
of the term "self-insurance" will be best understood by an example.

Assuming interest at 4 per cent., and the American Table of Mortality (that prepared by Mr.
Sheppard Homans, on the experience of the Mutual
Life Ins. Co. of New York), the annual premium
for a whole-life policy of $1,000, at the age 40,
apart from the addition or "loading" for expenses,
is $22.36. This is the mathematical equivalent,
under the assumptions, to the series of net natural
increasing premiums, beginning with $9.42. But
if $22.36 is paid instead of the $9.42, it is important to remark that *the risk to be borne by the company on the policy is diminished.* It is supposed,
for the sake of simplicity, that the death-claim, if
it occurs, is settled at the *end* of the year, till which
time the provision for it paid or in hand, at the
beginning of the year, is on interest at 4 per cent.
If only the natural premium of $9.42 has been paid,
amounting to $9.79, at the end of the year, and the
party dies, the other members, that is, the company,
has to pay $1,000—$9.79=$990.21. If $22.36 has
been paid, amounting to $23.25 at the end of the
year, then the company has to pay but $1,000—
$23.25=$976.75. Hence the risks in the two cases
are in the ratio of 990.21 to 976.25, and *if the former
is called an insurance of $1,000*, then the latter is

an insurance of only $\dfrac{976.75}{990.21} \times 1000 = 986.41$. And
the difference, $1000 - 986.41 = 13.59$, is not insured by the company. But since the heir receives it as part of the death-claim, it is reasonable to say that the party *insured himself* to that extent. Thus, on account of the increase of the artificial net premium over the natural one of the year, for the amount insured, the business of the year necessarily resolves itself into two generically distinct transactions. First, the party buys of the company an insurance of $986.41, for which he pays the natural net premium of $\dfrac{986.41}{1000} \times 9.42 =$ 9.29. Consequently the balance of his premium, $22.36 - 9.29 = 13.07$, is a mere savings bank deposit, which, increased at 4 per cent., makes up $1,000, by *self-insurance* or *accumulation*.

If the death does not occur, then the $13.59 must remain in the company's hands, by mathematical necessity, as well as legislative enactment, to diminish future risks, which is the same thing as to provide against future deficiencies of the level premium. It is, in fact, a trust fund, accepted on the condition that it shall count on the death claim, if it occurs, and remain on hand to diminish the future risks, if it does not. It is not available for a claim on any other policy.

The effect of paying the $22.36 the second year,

is, that the company will have \$35.95, which, at
the end of the year will amount to \$37.39, instead
of the \$10.01 which it would have had if only the
natural premium for \$1,000 had been paid.   Hence
the risks this second year are in the ratio of 989.99
to 962.61.   Consequently, the insurance done by
the company is $\frac{962.61}{987.99} \times 1000 = 972.34$, and the balance, \$27.66, is the *self-insurance*, reserve, or
"value of the policy," at the end of the second
year.*

It would be better, always, to call this the *self-
insurance* value of the policy, to distinguish it from
another very important and different thing, which
is properly the *insurance value* of the policy, that
is, the sum which, paid in advance, under the
assumptions, would exactly pay for all the insurance which *the company* is to do under the policy,
as distinguished from that which the party is to do
himself.

It will readily be perceived that the ratio in which
the two processes of insurance and self-insurance
or accumulation, enter into the business of each
year can be as easily and accurately precalculated
as anything else relating to the business, so that
there is no excuse for keeping mixed up in mystery two things that are essentially different, and

---

* The results would be slightly different by the Actuaries' Mortality,
for which see Appendix.

both perfectly simple and intelligible by themselves. And since the working expenses of a life-insurance company are much larger than those of a savings bank having the same amount of funds on hand, it is quite obvious that while the various premiums paid are divided between insurance and self-insurance in exceedingly different ratios, only the wildest wreck of equity can result from assessing the expenses upon the premiums paid. Much less would come from assessing them on the amount of the policy, but that would only about half correct the blunder in the average case. There can be no reasonable correction till the insurance is carefully distinguished from the self-insurance on every policy, and the significance of the "insurance value" of every policy is recognized,—in short, till the insurance is treated on insurance principles, and the accumulation on savings bank principles.

The peculiarity by which American is distinguished from British life insurance, is the more distinct and pronounced recognition on this side of the water of the reserve on each and every policy as a trust fund, applicable only to the claim on that particular policy. Or what is the same thing, the recognition of the aggregate net value of all the outstanding policies as a matured liability to the living policy-holders. To this the American companies are more or less bound by State law, while the British are left entirely to be a law to themselves.

The practical difference is one of life and death, as a general fact. An American company may die, but unless it criminally evades the law, it will die solvent,—a much milder calamity than that which overtakes about nine-tenths of the British offices. This means that it will be able to return to the policy-holders the trust fund, or accumulation. It will only be unable to continue its insurances. Even this mild calamity which is now impending, more or less, over all our offices, might be averted by heroically correcting the blunder of mixing things which are not homogeneous.

Were the business of life insurance in this country practically in the hands of scientific men, the practical errors would soon be corrected. What little science has been turned in this direction is all right, but it is very little regarded. The man who controls the biggest pile of policy-holders' money, regards scientific men not as guides but tools. If one does not suit him, he tries another. As to the men who control the smaller piles, they look to the bell-wether, and not to the stars, for their courses. The only hope of improvement is in the growing intelligence of the people themselves.

It is only by the cultivation of thought, truth, and justice among mankind, that useful institutions can be kept from decay. There was included in life insurance at the start, too much falsehood, not by evil intention, but want of thought. It was immensely increased on this side of the water, when we made our policies, as we had good reason to do, more *accumulative*, and this was for want of thought. But a falsehood which creeps in unwittingly may be adopted by men of mercenary motives, and used wittingly, with high pretensions, for a mean purpose. This has been done. Its tendency is but too plain. Let us suppose an institution, intended to promote a universal regard for truth, should use a lie to frighten people from lying; plainly, whatever might be its temporary success, it could not be permanent. Organized falsehood, no matter how good its motive, grows into certain failure. Power without justice, proves its own executioner. Truth is, after all, the vital force of society, transmuting itself into the forms of justice, order and happiness. Falsehood, father and mother of ignorance, is the principle of social disease and death. Nothing which is good for society courts concealment. Life insurance will be good for society, when the policy conceals nothing, but speaks so plainly on every point, as to leave the agent no opportunity to lie, if so disposed, nor the policy-holder any claim to be dissatisfied, unless it is with himself.

The writer has discussed this subject in various journals, as different points and aspects of it have arisen during the last three years, and published a set of precalculated working tables,

with an introductory explanation, designed to give
information to the ordinary, as well as the scientific
reader. It appears to him that the happiest of
these attempts to popularize a very dry though important subject, will be more useful to the reader
who wishes to get at the marrow and merits of it,
than any set treatise. He has, therefore, arranged
in the following pages, a selection from them. The
algebra, which is more or less sparsely scattered
through them, may be skipped without losing the
pith of the matter. It is not to be supposed that
the ordinary reader will in all cases become con-
vinced that the solution of the difficulty here proposed, is the correct one, or the best that can be.
He will wish to hear the other side, but he will
not fail to notice this, that a liberal prize is offered to any one, who within a year will produce a
justification of the practices of the life insurance
companies, by me stigmatized as errors and blunders. The companies that persist in these errors
and blunders, have a pretty strong inducement to
add to this prize, should there be need of it.
Therefore, if the attacks I have herein made on the
received and long practised mode of doing the business, are not fully answered and repelled before a
year comes round, from the date of that offer, the
public will certainly know that it is because science
and money can't do it.

Chapter II.

MASSACHUSETTS NON-FORFEITURE LAW.

The writer had not been long in the office of Insurance Commissioner in Massachusetts, before he was struck with the fact that the penalty of forfeiture in different companiês, and often for different members of the same, was very different. Many companies took half the premium in the note of the party insured. In case of forfeiture this note was never collected, so that the company, to which the note was precisely the same as cash, in fact paid a cash surrender value, equal to the amount of outstanding premium notes, while to the party who had paid the whole premium in cash, it would pay no surrender value at all, either in cash or further insurance, in case of non-payment of premium when due! This glaring violation of equity was urged upon the attention of the legislature, till the result was the Act of 1861, regulating the forfeiture of policies. For the want of any knowledge or recognition at that period, of "insurance value," as the proper basis of "surrender charge," the Act adopted the received absurd rule of making it a percentage of the reserve, limiting it to one-fifth,—except so far as the reserve consisted in notes, which were left as cash surrender value, without charge. For this, and other reasons, that Act is very crude, and inadequate to its purpose. It fails sufficiently to protect policies of large cash accumulation, and equally fails to interpose a reasonable or sufficient barrier against early lapse. In this respect it has the very fault of the premium-note system. It exacts too much of the company in the early stage of a long policy, and too little in all other cases. All that can be said for it is, that the Commissioner and the legislature met a strong demand for regulation in the best way they then knew how. The strength of the case will appear from the following extract from the Fourth Annual Report of the Massachusetts Insurance Commission, 1859 :—

Public opinion has been too unenlightened to oblige the directors of these institutions to follow any particular rule for avoiding over-accumulation, and, left to themselves entirely, they seem in numerous cases to have attempted to take two courses at once—on the one hand endeavoring to attract business by declaring large dividends, and on the other to provide for safety by not paying them for a long time if at all. Not to speak of other faults, this plan has the double disadvantage of not being either decided in its tendency or intelligible to the public.

There are two general plans adopted for avoiding over-accumulation. One is to diminish the assets, and the other to increase the liabilities. The former, when the surplus is fairly divided among those who have contributed to produce it, is a very plain and satisfactory process, as well as perfectly safe, if not carried beyond the right mark. The latter, which seems to have grown out of the desire to divide and hold on at the same time, a feeling nearly as old as life insurance itself, is not so plain and is attended with some difficulties.

According to this plan, when a mutual company finds itself in possession of much more than enough to reinsure its risks, or in other words, to meet its matured liability on them, it increases that liability at once by persuading or compelling its members to insure more, the additional sum insured being that of which each member's share in the dividend is the single premium, at his present age. So far as the members are concerned, if they do not want the ready money and do want the additional insurance, this would be all very well, provided the company gave an independent policy, but it attaches the addition to the policy already in force which is conditioned on the punctual payment of its annual premium. If that premium should be paid punctually for twenty years, and one payment be then omitted, not only the policy would be forfeited, but the additional insurance, though fully paid for by what was the same as cash, and now increased in value, would go to nothingness with it. The absurdity of having the forfeiture of an annual-premium insurance work the forfeiture of one on which the premium has all been paid down, is too flagrant to need dwelling on, yet it is the practice in several of the companies doing business in this State. The excuse offered for this palpable injustice is, that every insuree is made aware, before taking his policy, that such is the condition of forfeiture, both of it and all the additions that may be made to it. If a person in such circumstances, commencing a life-long experiment, does not misunderstand the conditions of the policy, he may misunderstand his own strength, and may be very unwise in piling up penalties to be visited years hence on his want of punctuality. Why should the company invite him to do it? In regard to the forfeiture of the original policy itself by non-payment of premium, we shall have more to say by and by, but in regard to new single premium insurance, or reversionary dividend, whether liable to forfeiture or not, if imperative upon the company, at the option of the insured, it involves the absurdity of insuring without selection. The worst lives only will choose reversions, and this must tend to injure the company. Only where it is compulsory on all the members to accept reversionary dividends, will the average vitality of the members be secured for this class of insurance, and even in that case, if, as is sometimes supposed, the beneficial effect of selection wears out, it must be worse for the company than to return the surplus. It is true that by this sort of addition to the policy, while the liability to forfeiture is not much diminished, the company will gain much more if it takes place. Ought that to be a motive with an institution which claims to be rather philanthropic than mercenary?

The companies that have resorted to this plan of avoiding surplus or preserving the proper relation of assets to liabilities, and the sums they have added to the amount insured by annual premium, are as follows:—

State Mutual, Worcester, ...	$84,180 86
National, Vermont, ...	16,144 24
Manhattan, New York, ...	137,515 00
Mutual Life, New York, ...	3,111,354 69
Total, ...	$3,349,194 79

Here is an aggregate of more than three millions of dollars of insurance for which the companies have been paid in full, every dollar of which is liable to be forfeited by the non-payment of premium on *other* insurance! The present value of this insurance has been carefully calculated by us, but has not been kept distinct from that of the policies to which it is attached. It probably exceeds one million of dollars. Except in the case of the Mutual Life Insurance Company of New York, it is all attached to whole-life policies. The reversionary dividends of the Mutual Life, to the sum of $13,-853.67, are attached to endowment policies, and are payable

with the policy. To the sum of $41,657.07, they are attached
to term policies, and though cast as reversionary, or at single
premium for the whole life, are payable at death only in case
the death takes place within the term for which the life is
insured in the policy. To illustrate : suppose the holder of a
seven-year policy, which has two years yet to run, is entitled
to $84.85, as his share of cash surplus. The company, in-
stead of paying it to him in cash, adds $200 to his policy, his
age now being 40, and $200 being the amount which a single
premium of $84.85 will insure, payable whenever death
occurs. But he must forfeit this *paid-up* policy of $200 by
not dying within two years! This may be no fault of his,
for perhaps he cannot help living. It may be considered a
trifling or impertinent question, but why should not the company either pay the $200 whenever the death occurs, having
received the full value for that insurance, or else give him the
value of $84.85 in insurance for the remaining portion of his
term ? This would require, for a single temporary premium
similarly loaded with their life premium, an addition to the
policy of $3,872.84. It is very true, and only fair to say, that
this company's practice is somewhat better than its principle,
for if at the close of the term policy the holder takes out a
new policy for the whole life—which we suppose he may do
if his health is sufficiently good—the company will add to it
the reversionary dividend attached to the former policy.

We have been the more particular to call attention to the
extreme case of these reversionary dividends, in the hope of
attracting more attention to the general question of the forfeiture of life policies by failure to pay the periodical premium
at the time specified in the policy. As we have already
shown, a mutual life insurance company partakes of the
nature of a savings bank. Money is deposited to be returned
certainly, but at an uncertain time. Therefore, taking one
policy with another, there must be a long process of accumulation, and the annual premium on a life policy, taken at any

age, must be much larger than is exhausted in paying for the insurance of any one of its earlier years. Hence at the close of any year, when the premium of the next year is due and not paid, there is always in the hands of the company a balance which it has not earned. If the insured pays his premium before the last minute of grace expires, the balance continues to be his, and his insurance is kept good; but if he does not, his balance goes to the company, by the conditions of the policy and the law of the land. He may have paid his premiums regularly for ten years and have several hundreds of dollars in the general fund, and yet because one hundred is not paid to-day, he may lose it all, and what is worse, if he dies, his widow may receive neither the amount insured nor the value of his policy. It would hardly be deemed fair to have one's note protested in a bank where he had funds deposited to several times the amount for the express purpose of paying it. Turning from the literal conditions of the policy to the reason and equity of it, we shall see that the analogy is sound, and that a policy ought not to become void for non-payment of premium till the sum already paid has been exhausted in temporary insurance, or in other words, till the policy has no longer any value, and nothing should be forfeited but the right to reinstate it. It would be penalty enough—if penalty is necessary to secure punctuality—to have it placed at the option of the company whether the policy should be restored to its character of a whole-life policy by the payment of the back premium and interest, after having sunk to that of a temporary policy by an omission of payment.

We do not think it would be a law impairing the just obligation of contracts,* but quite the contrary, which should enact that hereafter any policy issued by any company char-

---

* The Act finally passed applies only to policies issued after its date. Some, if not all the Massachusetts companies have voluntarily applied it to prior policies.

tered by authority of this Commonwealth, after lapse for non-payment of premium, should nevertheless be good against the company in case of death, should that event occur before the value of the policy, at the time the last premium was due should be exhausted in temporary insurance—the value of the policy and the term of the temporary insurance to which it shall entitle to be determmined by the rules adopted by the Insurance Commissioners, allowing 25 per cent. of loading on the net temporary premium. For example, in the registry in this office, of policies in force against the New England Company, policy number 2,893 was issued January 2, 1850, to a person then aged 50, insuring for life $5,000. Its net value, as appears by the registry on the 1st of November last, was $1,027.01. On the 2d of January last, when the premium was due and before it was paid, the value had diminished to $1,016.68. If the insured then paid the premium of the company, $235, he paid, as compared with the net premium adopted for this valuation, $56.12 as the "loading" for expenses, or 23.88 per cent. of his premium, and the balance, $178.88, went to increase the value of his policy, which became at once $1,195.56. When the next year's premium becomes due, January 2, 1860, the policy will have diminished in net value by $61.36, the net cost of the year's insurance, which the company has earned, and it will be then worth $1,134.20. Should the holder fail to pay the $235 of annual premium that day, he will forfeit to the company the $1,134.20, and if he dies the day after, his heirs will not have any legal claim to one cent of the $5,000. The officers of the company, as we all know, if the insured should seasonably request them, would do everything in their power to prevent the lapse, and would not refuse to lend the amount of the premium on the pledge of the policy. And after the lapse they would allow the policy to be reinstated, if the health should be good. But they are under no legal obligation to do this, and should the holder for any reason, or the want of it, allow the payment to be omitted and be overtaken by death, the officers would not feel themselves at liberty, however much disposed to do it, to pay either the loss or the value of the policy at the time of the lapse, though, having been over-paid by the " loading " for the expenses. The company has no more right in equity—apart from the letter of the contract—to hold the net value of the policy after refusing to pay the loss, than it has to rob the house of the deceased of an equal sum. Regarding the $1,134.20 as the gross or " loaded " single premium for a person 60 years of age, it is sufficient to insure $5,000 on his life for the term of six years and twelve days, and the company, not returning the value of the policy, would be no loser by paying the $5,000, should death occur at any time within that term. What we would most earnestly recommend is, that the company should be obliged by law to do it. Let the failure to pay the premium as stipulated only release the company from the obligation to insure beyond the time and amount already paid for. Apart from the consideration of justice to the insured, we believe policies under a legal provision of this kind would be greatly preferred, and would attract business to the companies issuing them. Profits caught by the trap of forfeitures frighten away ten times their amount, deterring the most prudent people from running the hazard of life insurance.

In 1870 this law, though somewhat popular, had become so vexatious to the executive officers of the companies, in several respects, that some of them applied to the writer to aid them in getting it amended. Having by this time become aware of the mistake in the surrender charge, and having always been aware of certain other troublesome imperfections in the law, he gladly undertook the task, and drafted the bill which will be found further on, for fixing a cash surrender value, with an adequate surrender charge, as a substitute for extended insurance. He understood the presidents of at least two companies, to approve this bill, and he expected their aid in recommending it to the legislature. But it would have the effect to prevent the agents receiving the exorbitant commissions they now do on certain classes of policies. This sealed its fate. The agents discovered its tendency, and raised so vigorous a howl that the presidents gave it no support, though they exhibited no animosity towards it. In spite of the active opposition, it passed the House of Representatives by a large majority. Its opponents, however, cunningly introduced into it an amendment, applying it to all companies doing business in the State whether chartered by it or not. This brought to the aid of the opposition in the Senate, an immense reinforcement. Judge McCurdy of Connecticut appeared as the lobby representative of the Mutual Life Insurance Company of New York, and produced great effect by the statement that Prof. Bartlett, the distinguished actuary of that company, had the subject of "surrender charge" in hand, and had arrived at results very different from those of Mr. Wright incorporated in this bill. These results would be published in due time, and he begged the Senate to postpone the subject till Prof. Bartlett's paper should be published. It was done, and that paper

2

has since been published and revised. The revised
form of it, with the writer's reply, will be found on
subsequent pages. Here follows the minority report of the Insurance Committee which introduced
the bill to the House,—a minority of *one*, which
will not probably have reason to be ashamed of its
report.

[House Document, No. 387, 1871.]

MINORITY REPORT.

The undersigned, a minority of the Committee on Insurance, asks leave to submit the accompanying Report and
Bill.   JOHN NEWELL.

A healthy man stands about 8 chances out of 1,000 of dying
within one year at the age of 27, about 9 out of 1,000 at 33,
about 10 out of 1,000 at 39, about 11 out of 1,000 at 43, 12 at
45, 13 at 47, 14 at 48, 15 at 49, 16 at 50, 17 at 51, 18 at 52, 30
at 60, 44 at 65, 65 at 70, &c.   Hence it costs eight times as
much to insure a given sum for one year at 70 as at 27.

If a mutual life insurance company of several thousand
members could be created, maintained and operated with no
other expense than the payment of death-claims, a healthy
man at 27 would need to pay only $8 to be insured for $1,000
for *one year;* and at 60 only $30 for the same.   But the man
at 27 wishes more than one year's insurance.   He does not
like to have the policy cease at a stipulated age, lest when
that time comes his health should be such that the company
will refuse to renew the policy.   Therefore he wishes to bind
the company to continue the policy as long as he pleases to
pay the premium.   If there were no necessary working expenses, and every member could be depended on to continue
paying his premium according to agreement during his whole
life, the man at 27 might begin by paying, for $1,000, $8 the

first year, a little more the second, and so on till at 33 he would pay $9, at 39 $10, at.70 $65, and at 99, if he should live so long, he would pay about $940.

But it is impossible to create or maintain a life-insurance company large enough to make anything *sure* without great expense, and the members cannot be depended on to persevere in paying premiums, especially *increasing* ones, unless they are to forfeit something besides the right to be insured by ceasing to pay. Hence the company charges a person aged 27 on a policy for $1,000 for the whole life, an annual premium payable during life of $15.56 for the insurance, and about $3.89 in addition for expenses, making $19.45. As to the $15.56, from what has been already said, it is plain that it will exceed the company's risk till the age of 49, or 22 years. If the party reaches 49 alive there must then be a fund on hand to the credit of his policy of $256.86. If he dies that year this fund goes to help pay the claim of $1,000, so that the other members have to pay only $743.14.

In fact, in every practicable form of insurance covering the whole life or a long term, the policy, historically considered, is a combination of a series of insurances by the company, with a series of *self-insurances*, or insurances by the party himself, effected either by his money or his note in the hands of the company. According to the Massachusetts rule of reserve, the relation of these two insurances, in the successive years of a policy for $1,000, entered at 27, and payable at death whenever it may occur, will stand as in the following table. It is assumed that no one can live beyond the age of 100, so that a whole-life policy becomes in fact an endowment policy, payable at 100, or previous death. Omitting, for brevity's sake, the intermediate years, the first and last years during which the policy *may* exist will have the two insurances in any year equal to $1,000, thus :—

YEAR, . .	1st	2d	3d	4th	5th
Insured by Co., Self-insurance, .	$991 76 8 24	$983 25 16 75	$974 47 25 53	$965 40 34 60	$956 04 43 96
	$1,000 00	$1,000 00	$1,000 00	$1,000 00	$1,000 00

YEAR, . .	6th	7th	8th	9th	10th
Insured by Co., Self-insurance, .	$946 38 53 62	$936 41 63 59	$926 11 73 89	$915 48 84 52	$904 50 95 50
	$1,000 00	$1,000 00	$1,000 00	$1,000 00	$1,000 00

YEAR, .	68th	69th	70th	71st	72d	73d
Ins. by Co., Self-ins., .	$85 58 914 42	$78 97 921 03	$73 84 926 16	$67 00 933 00	$54 02 945 98	$0 00 1,000 00
	$1,000 00	$1,000 00	$1,000 00	$1,000 00	$1,000 00	$1,000 00

This relation of insurance to self-insurance, it is to be remembered, is fixed by law. If the same policy had been payable at the age of 37 or previous death, the law would fix the relation of insurance to self-insurance on it, thus:—

YEAR, . .	1st	2d	3d	4th	5th
Insured by Co., Self-insurance, .	$919 70 80 30	$835 63 164 37	$747 57 252 43	$655 34 344 66	$558 68 441 32
	$1,000 00	$1,000 00	$1,000 00	$1,000 00	$1,000 00

YEAR, . .	6th	7th	8th	9th	10th
Insured by Co.,	$457 37	$351 13	$239 69	$122 75	$0 00
Self-insurance, .	542 63	648 87	760 31	877 25	1,000 00
	$1,000 00	$1,000 00	$1,000 00	$1,000 00	$1,000 00

If the policy, instead of being payable to the party himself if alive at the expiration of the term of 10 years, were only payable to his representatives in case of his death within the term, then the law would fix the relation of insurance by the company to the self-insurance, as follows:—

YEAR, . .	1st	2d	3d	4th	5th
Insured by Co.,	$999 37	$998 85	$998 43	$998 15	$998 01
Self-insurance, .	0 63	1 15	1 57	1 85	1 99

YEAR, . .	6th	7th	8th	9th	10th
Insured by Co.,	$998 03	$998 23	$998 61	$999 21	$1,000 00
Self-insurance, .	1 97	1 77	1 39	0 79	0 00

If we carefully consider these three contracts,—or rather two, for the first two are substantially alike,—we shall see that it is easy to calculate, at any point in the history of either, what it may be expected to contribute, on any assumptions, towards paying claims on other policies during its future course. The present value of all these normal contributions to the fund out of which the death-claims are paid, so far as the company, and not the claimants themselves, have them to pay,—may be called the *insurance value* of the policy, in distinction from the reserve or "net value" at the end of the policy-year, which is more appropriately the *self-insurance value*.

For example, since at 27 the chance of dying in a year is about eight out of 1,000, or strictly, by the legal assumption, 708 out of 88,434, the ten-year term policy which has a risk of $799.37 borne by the company will contribute $\frac{708}{88434}$ of $999.37 to death-claims on other policies, or $8. If the party lives another year, his policy in that year will contribute $\frac{714}{87726}$ of $998.85, or $8.13. If he lives a third year, his policy will contribute in that year $\frac{720}{87012}$ of $998.43, or $8.26, and so on.

On the endowment policy for ten years, the contributions to the death-claims on other policies in the same three years will be $\frac{708}{88434}$ of $919.70 the first year, $\frac{714}{87726}$ of $835.63 the second year, and $\frac{720}{87012}$ of $747.57 the third, that is in the three successive years, $7.36, $6.90, and $6.19. And in the same way the first three contributions of the whole-life policy will be $7.94, $8, and $8.06. In the 69th year of the whole-life policy, if it should exist so long, the insured then being 95 years old, his policy will contribute to the death-claims on other policies $\frac{58}{99}$ of $78.97, or $46.14. This is paid thus: The net premium, $15.56, is added to the self-insurance fund of the previous year, making $929.98, which at 4 per cent. will amount to $967.17, from which, deducting the cost of insurance, $46.14, we have left $921.03, the self-insurance of the 69th year.

The present value of these normal contributions to pay the death-claims on other policies is ascertained thus : that of the current year is simply discounted at the assumed rate of interest; that of the second is multiplied by the present value of a dollar due in two years, and the product is multipled by the fraction expressing the chance of the party being alive to contribute in the second year. So of any other possible contribution. Thus the present value of the third contribution of the whole-life policy will be (at 4 per cent.) $8.06 \times .888996 \times \frac{87912}{88434}$ or $7.02; and the sixty-ninth contribution will be $46.14 \times .066,788 \times \frac{89}{88434}$, or 0.0031. If the present values of all the possible normal contributions towards the death-claims are thus found, the sums of them on the three policies above stated will be as follows: whole life, $189.40; ten-year endowment, $34.69; ten-year term, $76.86. These numbers appear as nearly as possible to measure the relative value of these three policies at the start to the company as an insurance company. They also measure relatively the interests the several policy-holders have in the enlargement and maintenance of the company as an insurance company. The annual premium paid for the whole-life policy of $1,000, at 27, is usually $20.93, for the ten-year endowment policy, $104.16, and for the ten-year term policy—in case such a policy is taken—$13 or $14. Nothing can be more obvious than that if these policies are made to contribute to the working expenses of the company, that is, to other expenses than the payment of policy-claims, in the ratio of their premiums, that a gross injustice is done to at least two of them, and especially to the endowment policy. Suppose the company, as often happens, has really consumed 20 per cent. of its premium receipts in expenses outside of policy-claims. Then if these expenses are assessed on the premiums, the holder of the endowment policy is made to pay $20.83 to the life-policy holder's $4.19; that is, he will have to pay a great deal more to sustain the company as an insurance company, while his interest in it as such is less than one-fifth of that of the life-policy holder. It is true, his interest in the company as a savings bank is greater, and precisely in the ratio of $80.30 to $8.24, if both policies are in their first year, and of $1,000 to $95.90 if both are in their tenth year. A savings bank will do pretty well if its management does not cost over one-half per cent. on the deposits, but it would not be much patron-

ized if it cost over one per cent., and certainly not at all if
the expenses were more than the interest. Now supposing
we assess one per cent. on savings bank deposit or self-insurance, the life-policy will pay on that amount eight cents, and
the endowment eighty cents, both being in their first year.
This will leave $24.14 to be assessed on their interest in the
company as an insurance company, that is, to be divided in
the ratio of $189.40 to $34.69, which will throw $20.40 on the
life-policy, and $3.74 on the endowment, thus making the life
policy's share of the expenses $20.48, and the endowment
policy's $4.54. Supposing both policies in their tenth year,
one per cent. on the respective savings bank deposits that
year would be $10 for the endowment policy, and 95 cents for
the life policy, leaving $13.19 to be assessed on the insurance
values, which are 0 on the endowment, and $200.65 on the
life. Hence the endowment policy in its last year, having no
interest any longer in the company as an insurance company,
but only as a savings bank, should pay only the $10, and the
life policy should pay 0.95+13.19=14.14. Thus supposing
the amount of the expense $25.02 for these two policies to be
the correct thing, the endowment policy is overcharged $17.09
the first year and $10.83 the last. But the expense would un-
doubtedly have been somewhat less than $25.02 chargeable
to the two policies, but for the unreasonable practice of allowing the agent a commission on the premium, rather than on
the insurance value, which is the true measure of the value of
the policy to the company, as an insurance company. These
insurance values being at the outset in the ratio of $189.40 to
$34.69, if the company could not afford to give more than 40
per cent. of the first premium to procure the life policy (and
considering the rate at which policies lapse, it does not give
much more than this when it gives 15 per cent. on the
first premium and seven and a half per cent. on each succeeding one), then it can afford to give no more than one and
a half per cent. of its first premium to get the endowment

policy. In other words, if the life policy is worth to the company as an insurance company, but $8.37, the endowment policy is worth only $1.53, these sums being nearly proportioned to the *present values* of what the two policies may be expected to contribute towards the payment of claims on *others*.

Again, if the $25.02 is assessed on the premiums, so that the life policy pays $4.19 and the endowment $20.83, it will readily appear that this is equivalent the first year, to assessing the savings bank deposit over 25 per cent. Thus,—

	Life Policy.	Endowment Policy.
Savings bank deposit, ...	$8 24	$80 30
Insurance value, ...	189 40	34 69

To produce the $4.19 for the life policy and $20.83 on the endowment by a percentage on the deposit and another percentage on the insurance value, both percentages being the same for both policies, will require the percentage of deposit to be 25.46, and that on insurance value to be 1.1046. Applying these percentages to the life-policy deposit and insurance value, we have—

On savings bank deposit, ...	$2 10
insurance value, ...	2 09
	$4 19

And applying the same percentages to the deposit and insurance value of the endowment policy we have,—

On savings bank deposit, ...	$20 45
insurance value, ...	38
	$20 83

2*

It does not seem necessary to pursue this line of illustration
any further to show the entire absurdity of assessing expenses
on the premiums, when in all practical cases they consist of
two distinct parts, never bearing a constant ratio to each
other, either in different years of the same policy, or the same
year of different policies. It is also plain that *time*, the future
as well as the present of any contract, must be taken into
account. The share which any policy has in the accumulated
fund is a known quantity, and cannot be justly dealt with
on principles that could not be tolerated in a savings bank.
The share which it has in the company as an insurance
company embraces all the possible future years covered by
the policy as well as the present, and is as calculable as the
reserve or the premium. The whole strength of a company
as an insurance company consists of the aggregate of these
shares. The only damage done to a company by the retirement of a member is the diminution of its insurance strength
thereby. This is very nearly in proportion to the insurance
value subtracted, and would be exactly so if policies were all
of the same amount. It will be readily seen why a company
can a little better afford to lose a given amount of insurance
value on one life than on two. It has no relation whatever
to the self-insurance fund withdrawn. Suppose at the end of
five years the three policies above explained should withdraw.
Relatively to each other the insurance strength they will sub-
tract by withdrawing will be,—

Whole-life Policy, ...	$192 60
Ten-year Endowment Policy, ...	13 74
Ten-year Term Policy, ...	46 14

The self-insurance fund on each policy at the same date is,

Whole-life Policy, ...	$43 96
Ten-year Endowment Policy, ...	441 32
Ten-year Term Policy, ...	1 99

It is considered by most sound and conservative companies extravagant to give for a whole-life policy a brokerage of more than forty per cent. of its first premium, and this would not be more than six per cent. of its insurance value. Hence after paying a surrender charge of $11.56, or sufficient to procure another policy restoring the full insurance strength to the company, the policy-holder may be allowed to retire, withdrawing his deposit of $43.96. Hence the surrender value of his policy is $43.96—$11.56=$32.40. The surrender value of the endowment policy on the same principles is $441.32—.82=$440.50. But the term policy has no surrender value, because the surrender charge is $2.77, which exceeds the self-insurance fund or deposit of $1.99. In the same way the life policy would have no surrender value at the end of the first year because the surrender charge would exceed the deposit. In other words if it costs six per cent. of its insurance value to obtain a policy, it is not worth obtaining unless it has or will soon have deposit or self-insurance value enough to refund this cost in case of discontinuance. This can never be the case with short-term policies, and this is the reason why the companies are so much less anxious to obtain this class of business. Long-term endowment policies—including ordinary life policies—may not have a self-insurance value the first year equal to the cost of obtaining them, and if all of them lapsed at the end of the first year the company would sustain a loss on them. But if only twenty per cent. of them, as is usual, fail to pay the second premium, the loss on that portion may be more than compensated by the insurance value of the other 80 per cent. which persist. There is good reason here for two practical rules : *first*, not to give the agent out of the first premium so much that the company can lose anything if the second should not be paid. *Second*, not to take any part of the *first* premium in *note*, and not afterward to take so much in a note that the outstanding notes can ever exceed the *cash* surrender value of the policy.

Taking for granted that the present legal requisition for reserve is correct, it will be apparent that the proposed act, giving the policy-holder a right, at the end of any policy-year, to withdraw his savings bank deposit or *self-insurance*, less six per cent. of the *insurance value* of his policy, presents two, and only two, questions :—

1. Whether insurance value is the proper base of surrender charge.

2. Whether six per cent. is sufficient to keep the company whole. In other words, whether such a percentage will replace the business.

It cannot be apprehended that any company will put in a plea for any other base than insurance-value, and least of all, that any one will attempt to justify the deposit itself as that base. It appears to be an inevitable conclusion from the position already assumed by Massachusetts law, requiring reserve by a certain rule, that insurance value, as above defined, is the true basis of surrender charge. The deduction* from the deposit to indemnify the company must be a percentage of its loss of this, and it must be a *maximum* percentage for the most perfectly insurable lives. If the law allows this charge in every case, the company is injured in none, for it thus retains out of the deposit enough to pay for fully repairing the breach in its *insurance* resources. It must be distinctly borne in mind that the self-insurance or savings-bank deposit of any member is not, under our law, whatever it may be under English law or want of law, an insurance resource. It cannot be touched—as an average fact—and the premiums are so large that it never needs to be touched, except for the claim on the policy itself.

It only remains to consider whether six per cent. of the insurance value is sufficient. It will certainly not be sufficient to pay for procuring short-term endowment policies, at the rates now paid for that class of business. But for life policies, considering that it requires nothing to be taken out of the premium itself, it surely ought to be sufficient, being equal to from 30 to 60 per cent. of the premium. Let us suppose a mutual company having $12,000,000 insured, the insurance value of which is $2,700,000, and the savings bank deposit or self-insurance is $1,400,000. If under the proposed law every member should withdraw, there would be left in the hands of the officers $162,000. But our law deems $100,000 sufficient to build a new company with. And new companies have been started successfully with that amount to be returned with its interest when it should be no longer needed. But in our reconstructed company the $162,000 would not have to be returned, being a pure bequest from the self-defunct company that preceded it. The new company could have no just reason to complain of the old one for carrying with it $1,238,000 of its own money.

The benefit to the company of such a law is that men will be more ready to take policies when they know that they can, should circumstances change, at any time retire on equitable terms. Other contingencies belong to human life besides the time of its cessation. The motive or necessity for insurance may cease at any time. The insurable interest is almost sure to cease between 70 and 80, should life last so long. Of nearly all the policies that can be supposed to enter that decade, it must become desirable that they should be equitably settled within it, even if death should not occur. In point of fact, under the most unfavorable circumstances for equitable surrender, or in other words when surrender has to be effected on terms always inequitable, the average life of the whole-life policy has been found to be not one-half of the expectation of life at the age of entry. This shows that in numerous cases the maintenance of the policy becomes undesirable. Yet notwithstanding this urgent demand for it, neither the law nor the companies have ever provided any equitable method of getting out of this life contract.

Life insurance has flourished in England for a century or

more without fixing on any uniform or intelligible principle the surrender value of a policy. The practice may be said to be to exact as a surrender charge a variable part of the self-insurance, but always sufficient to border on robbery. That the surrender value paid there, even by the best companies, is atrociously too low, is abundantly proved by the regular sale of old policies at auction in the London Exchange, where they seldom bring more than half the reserve or savings bank deposit which must exist in the company. As a proof of this deplorable traffic, take the following advertisement cut from the "London Daily News," of February 6, 1871:—

"IMPORTANT SALE OF 42 OLD LIFE POLICIES AND REVERSIONS.

"By order of the Executors of a Gentleman deceased.

"Messrs. Broad, Pritchard and Wiltshire are instructed to sell by auction, at the New Mart, Tokenhouse Yard, E. C., to-morrow, February 7, at 1, precisely, in 42 lots, the following valuable Old Life Policies, effected in the most substantial London offices, offering to life offices, reversionary societies, capitalists and others a first-class opportunity of investing:—

Date of Policy.	NAME OF COMPANY.	Pres't Age of Life.	Premium.	Bonus Added.	Sum Assured.
1844	Law Life, . . .	48	£22 13 4	£314 0 0	£1,000
1834	Law Life, . . .	64	25 10 10	58£ 0 0	1,000
1829	Law Life, . . .	78	31 8 4	926 0 0	1,000
1846	Law Life, . . .	60	30 13 4	324 0 0	1,000
1839	Law Life, . . .	57 & 52*	15 15 8	258 0 0	400
1834	The Mutual, . . .	77	34 6 8	808 0 0	1,000
1838	The Mutual, . . .	66	13 18 4	315 0 0	500
1837	Law Life, . . .	69	122 13 4	2,198 0 0	4,000
1827	The Equitable, . .	76	28 11 0	965 0 0	1,000
1840	The London Assurance,	68	30 15 10	—	1,000
1834	The Amicable, . .	77	16 17 6	67 10 0	500
1824	Norwich Union, . .	67	6 3 9	90 0 0	300
1829	The Mutual, . . .	87	5 3 9	186 0 0	250

* Joint lives.

Date of Policy.	Name of Company.	Pres't Age of Life.	Premium.	Bonus Added.	Sum Assured.
1837	The Economic, . .	78	£26 14 2	–	£500
1835	Law Life, . . .	57	22 13 4	£515 0 0	1,000
1838	The Minerva, . . .	83	9 2 0	113 0 0	200
1838	The Sun, . . .	76	18 16 3	124 0 0	500
1833	The Alliance, . . .	70	16 13 4	230 0 0	1,000
1840	The Equitable, . .	60	21 7 0	478 0 0	800
1843	The Westminster, .	52	34 10 0	195 0 0	1,500
1829	The Imperial, . .	79	12 18 0	113 0 0	410
1843	The Atlas, . . .	72	17 18 9	235 0 0	500
1832	The Crown, . . .	75	8 19 6	100 0 0	300
1841	The Sun, . . .	64	26 8 6	205 0 0	1,000
1841	The Sun, . . .	64	26 8 6	205 0 0	1,000
1831	The Rock, . . .	70	27 5 10	698 0 0	1,000
1843	The Victoria, . .	58	12 12 9	113 0 0	500
1825	The Guardian, . .	80	2 17 –	35 0 0	100
1839	The Mutual, . . .	71	17 18 8	349 0 0	525
1844	The Mutual, . . .	77	11 17 1	170 0 0	250
1859	The Victoria, . .	47	7 19 6	–	300
1855	Liverpool and London, .	44	12 15 0	80 0 0	500
1859	Liverpool and London, .	44	10 10 0	83 0 0	500
1852	The Union, . . .	66	12 9 0	76 0 0	300
1852	The European, . .	72	16 10 9	–	300
1858	The Britannia, . .	54	7 10 5	–	500
1825	The Atlas, . . .	69*	–	–	750
1866	The Gresham, . .	38	5 13 2	–	200
1867	The Gresham, . .	38	5 16 6	–	200
1868	The Gresham, . .	38	5 16 6	–	200
1868	The Gresham, . .	38	5 16 6	–	200
1846	Law Life, . . .	73†	16 10 9	499 0 0	–

" The absolute reversion to the sum of £1,000 sterling, receivable on the death of a lady now aged 66 years, secured upon real estates in the county of Oxford.

" Particulars and conditions of sale may be had of Messrs. Pawle and Fearon, Solicitors, 11, New-inn; of Messrs. Rickards and Walker, Solicitors, 29, Lincoln's-inn-fields, W. C.; of Alfred Watson, Esq., Solicitor, 12, Fenchurch-street, E. C.; at the Mart; and of the auctioneers, 28, Poultry, E. C."

* Policy and reversion.
† The life interest of the last life is the sum of £2,736 16s. 11d.

. English law, to prevent speculation or gambling on human life, does not allow a policy to be issued without an insurable interest at the start, but it allows it to be maintained after the insurable interest has ceased to exist, and to be transferred for a consideration to a third party, who may maintain it as a matter of pure speculation, thus having a pecuniary interest to be advanced by the *death* rather than the life of the party insured. This was undoubtedly the case with this " gentleman deceased," who had picked up these forty-two old life policies at auction, bidding a little more for them than the surrender values which the companies were willing to pay. It would be interesting to know how much this gentleman gave for these policies and how much he would have been grieved if any of the insured had died between the date of the purchase and that of his own death. Translating pounds into dollars, we know that his interest in the immediate termination of the forty-two old lives was $192,782, which the companies were ready and able to pay on proof of death. So far as we know, not one of the insured could benefit him a shilling, or be anything but an expense to him, by continuing to live. His annual expense on them, all alive, was $3,825.80. Surely this deceased must have been very much of a " gentleman " while he lived if his extensive speculation in life policies did not occasion some uneasiness or nervousness among these forty-two persons, most of them old enough to have nerves.

The chief point of interest in regard to this lot of policies is their market value as compared with their self-insurance value. The latter at 3 per cent. would be $113,713, and at 4 per cent. $105,725. The insurance value of the whole would be at 4 per cent. $37,679.40; and considering 6 per cent. of this a sufficient surrender charge, we have $105,725— $2,260.76=$103,464.24, as what the companies could afford to give on the surrender of these policies, if they had no more than a 4 per cent. reserve. What they may have cost the

" gentleman deceased," supposing he had bought them just before he died, with no premiums paid since, is quite another matter. An article in the "British Assurance Magazine" for October, 1862, in discussing the market value of life insurance policies, gives from £119 4s. to £332 14s. as the price which may properly be paid for a policy of £1,000 entered at 20 and having paid 40 annual premiums of £17 5s. 10d., and of which the self-insurance value at 4 per cent. would of course be £564 10s. 11d. This would be equivalent to a surrender charge varying from 28.38 per cent. to 74.33 per cent. of the self-insurance value. We may therefore well suppose that 42 such old policy-holders having in British offices policies in which their self-insurance fund is $105,725, and on which they ought to realize in cash about $103,464.24, cannot get on the average so much as half that sum from the companies, but do obtain it in the auction mart out of the speculative proclivities of Hebrew or other gentlemen. This seems to be a state of things greatly to be avoided, and which is utterly inconsistent with the cherished idea of our own companies, that they are to a great extent savings banks.

No man at the outset of active life, the time when he most needs insurance, can say what his circumstances will be after thirty years or even ten years. A system by which he can be insured beyond a peradventure while he continues to desire it, and by which he can retire when he ceases to desire it, without having paid for much more than he has had, will have almost double the value of the present loose system, in which no one can know beforehand on what terms he can retire, and in which he is sure to pay more towards the working expenses of the company the less he is to be insured by it.

The appended bill is designed to secure to every holder of any policy hereinafter issued the right to retire from the company whenever he chooses, on equitable principles, and whenever it can be, consistently with justice to the company, to receive a cash surrender value which can be known at the time he takes the policy. The companies are now exceedingly injured in reputation, if not in funds, by the groundless complaints of those who retire after paying one or two premiums, very much dissatisfied because the whole of their premiums is not returned. A law fixing a just surrender value would prevent all this. The present law to regulate the forfeiture of policies does not at all meet the case of those who have ceased to need further insurance.

The "non-forfeiture law" (chapter 186 of the Acts of 1861) is defective in two respects:

1. It protects some policy-holders too much, and others too little or not at all.

2. In all cases where the party is insurable at the time of the lapse, there ought to be no deduction of foreborne premiums from the claim.

These defects have been vastly increased in importance by the great increase of endowment policies, to which when the term of the endowment is short, the law affords little protection. That law has, in fact, almost no merit except that *it means well.* At the time of its adoption there was nothing whatever to prevent a confiscation by the company of the whole of the self-insurance value or savings bank deposit on a policy, if a premium should fail to be paid when due. This was very hard on policy-holders who had paid a number of premiums in cash, and thus had in the company a cash deposit sufficient to pay for nearly as many more years of insurance as they had paid premiums. Moreover, it was obviously and, admittedly inequitable, because many of the best companies allowed the greater part if not the whole of this deposit, at the option of the insured, to remain in his hands in the shape of an interest-bearing note, and in that case if he forfeited his policy, he forfeited little or nothing more than his right to be insured further, on his paying for it. But so far as this deposit consisted in cash, the company had the policy-holder bound to forfeit insurance for which he had already paid. There could, of course, be no equity in doing worse by those policy-holders who had paid all cash than by those who had paid a part in notes, and there could be no justice in refusing to give as much insurance as had been paid for in cash. By the law the State simply intended to effect this equity and this justice in regard to all policies thereafter issued by corporations of its own make. But it failed to a very considerable and wholly unnecessary extent by the two provisions above named, to wit, deducting one-fifth of the net cash value from the premium for temporary insurance, and the forborne premiums with interest from the claim.

The effect of the first deduction is not to allow the company a sufficient compensation for the loss of a valuable contract, where an ordinary life policy, entered under the age of 50, lapses before paying its second or sometimes its third premium, and to allow it many times too much if it lapses after paying many premiums. The note-premium companies could not well object to this, because they took more than five-fifths of the net value of the policy at the end of the first year in a note at the beginning of it, whereas in point of equity, as between part-note and all-cash payers, they should never have taken any part of the first premium in note. In other words, whenever it will require the whole of the net value of any policy at the end of the policy year to replace it, if it should lapse, no part of the premium at the beginning of the year should be received in note. As a general and almost universal rule it costs money to get every policy into the company, and as much as the net value at the end of the first year, in case of an ordinary life policy, entered under about 50. This is not charged on the policy obtained as long as it stays in the company. The addition is a benefit to the whole company, and the whole company pays for it. But if the party wishes to retreat from his bargain, nothing can be plainer than that he ought to indemnify the company for the loss it sustains in losing him. In other words, he ought to pay enough to make his place good. Take for example a $1,000 policy for life, entered at 30. The net value of it at the end of the first year is $9.30, one-fifth of which is $1.86, or less than 9 per cent. of the first premium, whereas it costs from 15 to 40 per cent. of the first premium to obtain the policy. And if the company, having paid what it has paid for obtaining new business, had paid for obtaining each policy in the strict ratio of its value when obtained, that is, its *insurance* value, it would have unquestionably paid more than $9.30 for this one. For example, we will suppose it actually paid only $3.18 out of the first premium to obtain this policy, of which the first premium was $21.21, and that it paid $15.21 for obtaining a $1,000 ten-year endowment policy, entered at the same age, of which the first premium was $101.44, thus paying $18.39 for both policies. Inasmuch as the relative values of these two policies, are as $198 for the life, to $35.56 for the endowment, if the $18.39, had been paid for the two according to their value to the company, as an insurance company, $15.60 would have been given to obtain the life policy, and $2.79 only to obtain the endowment policy. It must be plain enough from this that one-fifth of the net value at the end of the year, in case of the life policy, is not a sufficient compensation to the company for the loss of insurance value by the lapse. It is very different with the endowment, where the insurance value to be lost is not one-fifth as great, and the net value at the end of the first year is eight times as great. If the endowment policy lapses after one payment, the law allows the company a compensation of $16.04 for a loss of insurance value which has now become only $30.64, while for the life policy it allows only $1.86 for a loss of insurance value which has now become $199.20.

In substituting term insurance for the original policy, as the law does, in case of lapse, the company never loses quite the whole of the insurance value. It loses nearly the whole of it on an ordinary life policy which lapses after only one premium is paid. And in this case, where it loses the most, the compensation is the least. In the case of the endowment policy at 30, lapsing the first year, after deducting one-fifth of the net value, there is $64.15 left, which will pay for a term policy for over eight years, and the insurance value of this is $51.70. That is, the company has been paid $16.04 to compensate it for the loss of $30.64 of insurance value, whereas, after deducting this from the net value, the term insurance substituted by the law more than replaces the insurance value by $21.06.

After an ordinary whole-life policy has paid a number of premiums, the deduction of one-fifth from its net value at the time of lapse, also becomes an extravagant compensation for the loss of the company. Such a policy, if taken under the age of 57, increases a little in regard to insurance value till the party reaches that age, after which the insurance value diminishes. For example, a life policy entered at 30, with an insurance value of $198 at the outset, has an insurance value of $229.80 at the age of 60. Its net self-insurance value is then $422.68, from which the law in case of lapse deducts $84.54, leaving $336.14 as a single premium of further temporary insurance. This will carry the risk nearly 12 years longer, and the insurance value of this paid-up term insurance is about $260, so that the company is paid $84.54 for a loss of insurance, which is, in fact, a gain of $30.20 on that score. There is in truth no end of the absurdities which flow from this making the surrender charge a percentage of the self-insurance value; and when it is applied to an endowment policy, lapsing after the net value becomes about half the sum insured, together with the reduction of the forborne premiums from the claim, it very nearly nullifies the intended protection. Thus the net value of the ten-year endowment policy, at

the end of the fifth year, is $440.83. Four-fifths of this is
$352.57, which is $12 more than the single premium for
life. at the age of 35. Hence, though the insurance value
has been increased from $10.18 to $141.98, *after* a present
to the company of $88.16, and the man has overpaid by
$100.16, for the full insurance of $1,000 for life, the *proviso*
about forborne premiums comes in, and if he should die
four years and a day after the lapse his heirs would receive $1,000—$568.04=$431.96!

All that can be said of this law is, that under. the circumstances, it was better than nothing. It will be seen at
a glance that any attempt to amend it so as to make it
apply equitably to all descriptions of policies must be attended with considerable practical difficulties and require
numerous rather complicated calculations. And after all,
it leaves a very large class of policy-holders, who, by a
change of circumstances have ceased to need or wish further insurance, tied up to receive nothing else.

An honest company cannot suffer, in the long run, by
leaving its policy-holders always free to withdraw in cash
their self-insurance or savings-bank deposit, subject to a
proper charge to compensate the company for its loss of
insurance value, and this charge should be a percentage of
its insurance value. Moreover, there can be no more effective safeguard against the mismanagement of the funds
entrusted to life-insurance companies, than to establish by
law the exact surrender value of any life-insurance policy
at the end of any policy year in its history. If a man by
self-destruction, military service or any other violation of
the conditions of his policy, forfeits his right to insurance
by the company, that is no reason why his widow should
be deprived of the sum wherein he had *insured himself.*
The cash surrender value should still be hers. The company, though it may have a right by the terms of the policy,
has no better moral right to divide it among the remain-

ing or surviving policy-holders, than it has to divide the clothes in which he died.

The passage of this Act would at once put a stop to the extravagant expenses which have grown out of the extravagant provision for expenses in the premiums of endowment policies. This sort of policy is very desirable for the insured if he can have it on reasonable terms, and nothing can be safer to the company than to give it to him on such terms. The net premium for a whole-life policy of $1,000 at 40 is $23.68, to which if 4 per cent. of the initial insurance value is added, making $33.18, this gross premium is ample. So the net premium at the same age for $1,000, payable at 50 or previous death, is $85.76, to which if 4 per cent. of the insurance value is added, making a gross annual premium of $87.62, the provision is as ample as in the other case, if only the expenses should be equitably assessed. But instead of the premiums above, the companies now offer the life policy for about $31.50 and the endowment policy for about $105. Unless this overloading of about $17 for every $1,000 by this class of policies is returned in dividends, the policy-holder is simply defrauded. He had by at least so much a year better have taken the life policy, and put the difference of the premiums in some other savings bank.

But as it may be said that all this is *theory,* let us now give a comparison of the status at the end of four years of two actual policies for $5,000 each, both entered at the age of thirty-eight, assuming the actual interest to be six per cent.

No. 1. An ordinary whole-life policy, with an annual premium of $146.50.

Cr.	By amount of four premiums,..	. . .		$679 30
Dr.	To amount of insurance, at cost,	.	$166 99	
	amount of dividends, .	. .	120 29	
	reserve, ...	.	276 08	
	balance, amount of expenses,	.	115 94	
				$679 30

No. 2. An endowment policy, payable at 60 or previous death. Ten annual premiums of $382.75 each.

Cr. By amount of four premiums,	. . .	$1,774 60
Dr. To amount of insurance, at cost,	. $147 48	
amount of dividends,	. . 242 31	
reserve, ...	. 1,130 75	
balance, amount of expenses,	. 254 06	
		$1,774 60

The expenses, supposing them the same each year, were, for the life policy $25.01, and for the endowment policy $54.78, per annum. For these expenses the premiums more than provided, the ordinary life premium leaving a margin over the net, at four per cent., of $36.41; and the endowment premium one of $84.23. But this sufficiency of margin cannot justify the company in charging more where less *is* insured, and less *is to be* insured. So far as the premiums are savings bank deposits it cannot be pretended that the company's service in conveying them from the person of the policy-holder to its own counter, and over it into the till, is worth more than two and a half per cent., nor that the manipulation of the funds after they are deposited should cost more than one-half of one per cent. per annum.

Let us suppose this to be settled in regard to both of these policies, and, moreover, that the charge on the life policy of $25.01 per annum was sufficient, reasonable and right. What ought to have been the charge each year on the endowment policy? The collection fee of two and one-half per cent., and one-half per cent. on self-insurance value would have been:—

YEAR.	Life Policy.	Endowment Policy.
1, ...	$3 99	$10 89
2, ...	4 33	12 27
3, ...	4 68	13 71
4, ...	5 04	15 22

This will leave the life policy chargable with an excess of $21.02 the first year, $20.68 the second, $20.33 the third, and $19.97 the fourth year. Now, in regard to the life policy, during the first year, the present value, at its normal cost, of all the insurance to be done upon it by the company in that and all its future years, is $1,138.50, while the present value in that year of all the insurance to be done by the company on the endowment policy is $380.40. These two sums represent as nearly as possible the respective interests of the two policies, at that time, in the company as an insurance company, in distinction from their respective interests in it as a self-collecting savings bank, which latter interests have been settled for above. Now if it is right that a policy having a stake in the company as an insurance company, valued at $1,138.50, should pay $21.02 for insurance expenses, the other policy, which has a stake valued at $380.40, should pay but $\frac{21.02}{1138.50} \times 380.40$ =$7.02, and by the same method, it should pay, in the succeeding years,—

Second year, ... $\frac{20.68}{1146.50} \times 352.20 = \$6.36.$
Third year, ... $\frac{20.33}{1157.75} \times 324.45 = 5.72.$
Fourth year, ... $\frac{19.97}{1163.25} \times 297.65 = 5.13.$

Hence, assuming the propriety of the charge on the life policy, the two policies should have been charged for expenses thus:—

YEAR.	LIFE POLICY.			ENDOWMENT POLICY.		
	On Savings Bank Deposit.	On Insur'ce Value.	Total.	On Savings Bank Deposit.	On Insur'ce Value.	Total.
1, . .	$3 99+	$21 02=	$25 01	$10 89+	$7 02=	$17 91
2, . .	4 33+	20 68=	25 01	12 27+	6 35=	18 62
3, . .	4 68+	20 33=	25 01	13 71+	5 71=	19 42
4, . .	5 04+	19 97=	25 01	15 22+	5 11=	20 33

3

If we restate the endowment policy at the end of four years with these corrected charges, we shall find the dividend materially increased, thus:—

Cr. By amount of four premiums, . . . $1,774 60
Dr. To amount of insurance, at cost, . $147 48
    Reserve, ... 1,130 75
    amount of expenses, . . 88 16
    balance, amount of dividends,. 408 21
    ————— $1,774 60

The previous statements being actual facts, we see from this statement that this endowment policy-holder was at the end of four years out of pocket $165.90. So much of his money was actually gone into the wildernesss for the want of a proper distinction between insurance and self-insurance. And it will be perceived at a glance that the case is put only too mildly, for on the average two and a half per cent. is great pay for carrying money to a savings bank.

It is not this particular wrong of a false assessment of expenses that it is proposed to remedy by legislation except indirectly. If such facts exist in the companies, there ought to be some convenient and just way of getting out. Now, suppose this endowment policy-holder grows tired of contributing to the expenses of a company out of all proportion to any benefits he is ever to derive from it, of a company in fact where he is hereafter pretty much to insure himself, how can he get out? His reserve or self-insurance is already $1,130.75, and the company, taking the unfortunate admission of the non-forfeiture law as it justification, will deduct one-fifth and give him the balance, $904.60. This means, that having been overcharged for expenses $165.90, while in the company, he shall be overcharged, let us see how much, for getting out.

First. Suppose the proper charge for the surrender of the

life policy at the same date, the end of the fourth year, when its self-insurance is $276.08 and its insurance value is $1,172, is $55.22, 20 per cent. of the former and $4\frac{71}{100}$ per cent. of the latter. Then the proper charge for the surrender of the endowment policy is $4\frac{71}{100}$ per cent. of *its* insurance value, which at the end of the fourth year is $270.90. That is, it should be charged $12.76, making its surrender value $1,118.02 instead of $904.60. Hence on this hypothesis it is overcharged in getting out of the company $213.42, which added to the overcharge while in the company makes a total of $379.32.

But *second*, suppose the proper charge on a life policy or any other is six per cent. of its present insurance value, then the life policy should be charged $70.32 and the endowment $16.25, so that on this hypothesis the overcharge on the endowment policy-holder to let him out of the company is $209.93, making the extent of his suffering only $375.83, and this is a dead loss of pretty nearly one premium out of four.

When we consider that the people of the United States, out of the eighty or ninety millions of life insurance premiums which they now pay yearly, are paying about fifty millions a year for endowment policies, or more than half, it must be seen that a great many people,—one quarter of a million at least,—have an interest in having this system changed, while a much smaller number have an interest in having it continue just as it is.

The individual constituents of the mutual life insurance companies in this country count up to half a million probably; and each on the average represents a considerable family. In *theory* the management of these great companies, now possessed of nearly two hundred millions of cash assets, is in the hands of these policy-holders, acting by means of about ten thousand officers and agents who are supported at an annual expense of about $12,000,000. These officers and agents may be policy-holders or they may not be. As a general rule their interest as office-holders must much exceed

their interest as policy-holders. How many of the policy-
holders, not office-holders, ever have any voice in their
appointment? For all practical purposes they are self-ap-
pointed. The government of these institutions, in which so
much of the future happiness of the country is wrapped up,
apart from some not very effective legislative enactments, is.
simply autocratic, *de facto.*

For the multitude of present policy-holders the legislature
can do nothing, for they are bound by contracts to which
they voluntarily assented. The obligations they have taken
upon themselves, however onerous or unfortunate, cannot be
impaired by statute so long as the companies stand ready to
fulfil all the obligations they assumed in the same instru-
ments. But in behalf of the future policy-holders, numbering
by tens and hundreds of thousands, born and unborn, the
legislature can prescribe that corporations created by itself
shall hereafter assume the obligation to deal on certain fixed
principles of equity with every member who chooses to retire,
by passing the following Bill :—

**AN ACT to fix the Surrender Value of Policies of Life In-
surance.**

Be it enacted, &c., as follows :—

SECT. 1. That under any policy of insurance on life, issued
after the tenth day of June, in the year eighteen hundred and
seventy-one, by any company chartered by the authority of
this Commonwealth, the holder thereof, on any anniversary
of its issue, shall be entitled to claim and recover of the company, any stipulation or condition of forfeiture contained in
the policy or elsewhere to the contrary notwithstanding, a
surrender value, to be determined as follows, to wit :—

SECT. 2. The net value of the policy at the said anniversary, the premium, if any is then due, not being paid,
shall be ascertained according to the combined experience
or actuaries' rate of mortality, with interest at four per
cent. per annum, and from such value shall be deducted

and cancelled any indebtedness to the company, or notes held by the company against the insured, and a surrender charge to compensate it for relinquishing the obligations of the policy to contribute towards the payment of future claims arising under other policies, to be ascertained as follows, to wit:—

SECT. 3. Assuming the rates of mortality and interest aforesaid, the present value of all the future contributions of the policy to pay death claims, or, in other words, of all the normal future yearly costs of insurance which by its terms it is exposed to pay, in case of its continuance, shall be calculated, and six * per cent. of this sum shall be the legal surrender charge, and the remainder of the net value of the policy, ascertained as aforesaid, after deducting this surrender charge, and any debts due the company as aforesaid, shall be payable in cash.

SECT. 4. No claim for surrender value under this act shall be valid, unless made within two years after the policy has ceased to be in force.

SECT. 5. Chapter one hundred and eighty-six of acts of the year eighteen hundred and sixty-one, shall not apply to any policy issued after the tenth of June, eighteen hundred and seventy-one.

After having faithfully fought for this bill up to its final defeat, at his own charges, without a particle of aid or comfort from the official persons who had invited him to undertake the warfare, the writer concluded to appeal to the people, the future policy-holders, themselves. The first thing to be done was to get up a set of policies of sufficient variety to accommodate all honest applicants for in-

* Amended to eight per cent. before passage.

surance, on such terms as to be safe for the company, sufficiently remunerative to the agent—supposing him a necessity of the case—and guarded against every contingency which a prudent man can foresee. This he did, taking the advice of the ablest practical experts as to the terms, precalculating every value which in its nature admits of pre-calculation, and so arranging the premiums payable on longer and shorter terms that one can never afford to put the difference between a higher and lower premium into an ordinary savings bank, but will take the shorter endowment in the life insurance company at the higher premium in preference, if he has the means. The working tables were published in 1872, with an explanation, under the title "Savings Bank Life Insurance." The only reason why the system was not popular with the companies—for some of them were eager enough to secure a monopoly of it—was that the agent would get the least on the policies that pay the largest premiums. He would be paid chiefly according to the "insurance value" of the policy, and not according to the premium, which includes more or less of savings-bank deposit, or *self-insurance*.

The life-insurance corporations, or autocracies, the moment they discovered the awful muddle they were getting into about short-endowment policies, fell back on the old ordinary whole-life policy, as the thing which ought never to have been departed

from, seemingly quite unconscious that they were
thus returning to the great original sin of the system—extending the insurance beyond the insurable
interest. In my "savings bank system," I took
some care to avoid this, and the reasons for it are
set forth in the following extracts from the Reports
of the Massachusetts Insurance Commission, with
perhaps more force than I can now command.

[From the Ninth Report, 1864.]

INSURABLE INTEREST.—In order to appreciate the comparative merits of different methods of life insurance, and the
value of the facts established by our vital statistics, it is important to have a distinct idea of what it is that is insured.
In other words, the first thing to be settled is, the nature of
the insurable interest in a life-policy. The insurable interest
is the money value of the life to a third party, and it can be
nothing else. The policy may be for less but not for more.
Says Judge Phillips :—" An exceedingly indulgent construc-
tion in favor of the sufficiency of an insurable interest in a
life, and in favor of the assignableness of life-policies not
based upon a substantive, distinct, valuable, appreciable, insurable interest, tends to convert such contracts into gaming
policies. Such a use of these insurances is subject to as great,
at least, if not greater, objections, than other species of gambling. For this reason, and for others relative to the influence
on morals and a temptation to crimes, life-policies ought to
contain provisions requiring notice of assignments to be
given to the insurers, and allowing to them the election either
to assent to the assignment, or to redeem the policy on reasonable terms." (Phillips on Ins., Vol. I., page 60.) Nothing
can be more just than the doctrine here laid down. A creditor can justifiably insure the life of his debtor only for the

purpose of securing his debt, and to the amount necessary
for that purpose. But a bad debt cannot be turned into a
good one in this way. If there is no probability that the
debtor will pay in case he should live long enough, then there
is to the creditor no insurable interest in the life, and the policy would be only a temptation to the crime of destroying it.
Insuring an unproductive life is like insuring unsalable goods
against fire. In either case the company, in effect, offers a
reward for the event insured against, only stipulating that
the agency producing it shall be so strictly concealed as to be
incapable of legal proof. On the principle that any creditor
may insure the life of any debtor, without regard to the value
of the life as a means of discharging the debt, the keeper of
a grog-shop, in despair of getting pay for the liquor which
had already destroyed the productive power of his customer,
might get the customer's life insured for a sufficient sum, and
hasten to establish a claim against the company by continuing
to furnish liquor. We have read of a case resembling this in
Denmark, and something, too, much like it, has occurred
nearer home. To make an insurable interest, the life of the
insured must have a money value to the party in whose favor
the policy is made. If a debt is already worthless, the life
of the debtor is of no value to the creditor, and there is no
interest in it to be insured, any more than if the debt did not
exist. So if the life of a husband or father contributes nothing, in a pecuniary way, to the maintenance of the wife or
the children, it is not justly insurable for their benefit, no
matter how great the loss of his life might be to them in point
of love. There is no money value for the affections. (See
Dickens, in the case of John Edward Nandy and Plornish,
and other novel authorities, *passim.*) A policy of insurance
on the life of a beloved relative, when there is really no insurable interest—that is, where the life is a pecuniary burden
rather than otherwise, if not felt to be so—is a very awkward
and uncomely piece of gambling. Probably very few poli-

cies are taken which have this character at first. But the subject of a policy may lose the insurable interest which it had at
first. If the premium for the entire life was paid at first, the
case presents no difficulty. The loss* has already occurred, and
the indemnity, already paid for, awaits the stipulated condition
of its becoming due. But if the premium is payable annually,
we may ask, in the light of the passage above quoted from
Judge Phillips, why, after the insurable interest has ceased
beyond any chance of recovery, the insured or anybody else
should be required or even permitted to pay further premiums.
At any rate, if the company, in the case of the assignment of
a policy where the insurable interest may have ceased, should
have the opportunity to redeem it at a reasonable rate, should
not the insured also have the liberty to stop paying for further
insurance on a life which, though likely to last long enough,
has ceased to have any money value or insurable interest?
Nine-tenths of the life-policies are made by their terms to
cover a period of life which, if reached, is in all but exceedingly rare cases, wholly destitute of the insurable element.
You might almost as rationally insure for a given sum a
wooden house for one hundred years, knowing that after
three-quarters of that time it would be utterly uninhabitable.
We are not objecting to the right of the party, having taken a
policy covering the whole life, and paid a higher premium on
that account during all the really insurable years, to carry the
contract through, but only to the reasonableness of making
such a contract at first.

It is not very difficult to see why people have taken, and
are ready to take, policies on their entire lives. Full of ac-
tivity at the outset of life, men have very dim perceptions of
the nature of old age. They expect to be useful, and to have
others dependent upon them until they die, be it early or late,
and they dread to have the insurance provision just a little
too short. The probability of such an occurrence every man
of course overrates in his own case. But as the second child-

3*　　* Of premium.

hood approaches, the failing powers begin to excite presentiments of a new condition, and though the man may see that he has contracted for something he will soon cease to need, he feels obliged, by the heavy penalty under which he is bound to the company, to go on and nurse a bad investment. Yet heavily as old whole-life policy-holders always have to pay to be released from their obligation to continue their premiums, a very large portion of them discontinue about the time when the insurable interest in their lives ceases. So few, indeed, have continued through life, that the combined experience of the English companies is altogether deficient in authority, as a law of mortality, beyond the age of seventy. Beyond that age, the scale of decrement is obliged to rely on the vital statistics of general population, and as the law of mortality is demonstrably different for different classes of population, the probability that the old age of insured lives corresponds with that of the general population is not a very satisfactory one. In insuring beyond seventy, the companies are acting comparatively in the dark, and this it is that justifies premiums so greatly redundant during the earlier years of the policy. Provision enough must be made against an unexplored period of life, *which, taken by itself, no company, not specially devoted to gambling for its own sake, would ever think of insuring.* We might, if time and space permitted, derive a practical illustration of the insecurity of life insurance for the advanced ages of life, from what has happened during the past year to the oldest life insurance company in the world, the Amicable Society, of London. It has been discussing the question whether to amalgamate or liquidate, the new business having ceased, the expenses being stereotyped, and the reserve fund not being sure, in the apprehension of the ablest actuaries, to meet the death-claims as fast as they may fall due. It is needless to say that no life insurance office deserves to exist unless it has a reasonable probability of carrying all its existing contracts through, without the aid of new ones. It is enough to say, that in all that part of life extending from the age when insurance begins to be desired to the age when insurable interest generally ceases, we proceed on probabilities amounting nearly to mathematical certainty; beyond that, we go by conjecture and experiment. By the Act of 1861 regulating the forfeiture of life insurance policies, the objectionable feature of insuring beyond the insurable interest is partly remedied, so far as concerns policies since issued by companies chartered in this State. That is, it is put in the power of the policy-holder himself at any time to set a limit to the insurance without forfeiting the value of his policy. But a policy may still be maintained at the pleasure of the insured, or his assignee, till the life terminates. The expediency of limiting all life insurance by the contract to a certain age is yet to be considered in this progressive country. It seems to us, on a careful consideration of the experience of the companies which we have observed for the last five years, as well as that of several of the larger American companies prior to that time, that premiums might be considerably reduced with safety on policies not extending beyond the age of seventy, and that with a proper and practicable economy as to expenses, a company can safely issue endowment policies, payable at the age of seventy or on previous death, the annual premiums charged for which up to the age of forty or perhaps fifty, need not exceed those charged for whole-life policies. Of course we do not say the dividends of surplus would be so large. If the policies do not extend indefinitely, and the undetermined hazard of extreme old age is not undertaken, it will do to assume a rate of interest not so much below that of present safe investments. At any rate, within the fairly insurable ages we are in a fair way to obtain a reliable scale of the decrement of insured life, and when it is once obtained, the practice can be made more closely to correspond with it than whole-life insurance can safely with a scale which is so largely hypothetical as the present.

[From the Tenth Report, 1865.]

We remarked six years ago, in our Fourth Report, page 27: "Of the insurance on life, a part consists of policies for definite short terms of from six months to fourteen years, and some of such temporary insurances coupled with endowment, or the payment of the amount of the policy to the insured himself, in case he survives the term. The latter are called endowment policies, and present the double attraction of providing for dependents in case the insured should be cut off during his active years, and providing against dependence in case he should reach old age. If the public were better aware of these advantages, this class of policies could not fail to become more popular." The public seems still unaware of the advantages of temporary insurance, especially of terms sufficiently extended to cover the whole of the active or productive period of life. It seems to be very generally believed that if a term policy should be outlived all the premium paid for it would be thrown away. This seems to be the reasoning of people who do not regard their fire insurance premiums as thrown away when their houses have not been burned. A man aged 30 ought to be able to get a policy of $1,000 for a term of 40 years by paying at least $4 per annum less than for his whole life; that is, the company can well afford to make that reduction in consideration of the limit. Four dollars per annum accumulated at six per cent. for forty years will amount to $619. But if he pays it to the life insurance company in order to have the policy extend over the whole life, and he is in sound health at the end of forty years, the company will not give him $619 as the surrender value of his policy, its value at four per cent. being only $594.38. But suppose he has taken the long-term policy, investing year by year the $4 difference of premium, and dies at the end of 35 years. Then his heirs get the amount of the policy, $1,000, the same as if the policy had covered the whole life, and also $445.72 the then amount of the investment outside. If he had paid the whole-life premium, his heirs would get nothing outside. It will be said that the whole-life policy will get a larger dividend than the long term, but this will only partially compensate the loss, for a life insurance company is always unprofitable as a mere savings bank, on account of its necessarily large expenses. But though the advantage of temporary insurance for long terms, is so little recognized either by the public or the officers of companies, when considered separately, it is rapidly growing in favor when coupled with endowment, and of course with the best of reasons, so far as the companies are concerned. It is safer for the company, the premium being properly cast, because its bet is always partially hedged. And the insured never thinks any of his premium thrown away, because, if the sum insured is not paid to his heirs he gets his endowment, and *vice versa.*

The general increase of this class of policies is very remarkable. We give below the progress of the three classes of policies, in a comparison of the number and amount of each outstanding on our registry for the last six years.

YEARS.	WHOLE LIFE.		SHORT TERM.		ENDOWMENT.	
	Number of Policies.	Amount Insured.	Number of Policies.	Amount Insured.	Number of Policies.	Amount Insured.
1858,	38,231	$107,659,465	3,999	$7,833,830	272	$988,900
1859,	44,593	123,913,596	3,645	7,574,974	369	1,252,256
1860,	51,230	142,176,279	3,446	7,148,114	668	1,974,437
1861,	53,348	144,258,449	2,945	6,267,475	846	2,417,653
1862,	71,425	189,494,396	2,950	5,810,250	1,567	3,958,437
1863,	92,083	245,525,587	2,741	5,751,153	3,119	8,448,450
1864,	136,565	357,304,512	2,990	6,431,974	7,007	18,833,703

Relatively to the whole amount insured, the short-term policies are rapidly decreasing. But the whole-life policies

have increased at an average ratio of twenty-two per cent.
per annum, and the endowment policies at an average ratio
of about sixty-three per cent. If this difference in the rate of
increase should be maintained for ten years there will be as
much insured on endowment policies as on whole-life policies. And when we consider the greater acceleration of the
endowment business, and the sound reasons for it, we may
expect that in another ten years very few whole-life policies
will be issued. This change will greatly promote the health,
prosperity and usefulness of the business.

It seems proper in this connection to call attention to the
real nature and use of life insurance. Any policy of insurance is in fact a bet. Its only justification is, that it is betting
made useful. The condition of its usefulness is, that it equal-
izes misfortunes or losses. An insurance on life does nothing
for the individual who dies. If nobody else loses pecuniarily
by the death, there is no more utility in the policy than in any
other bet. In fact, it is then no better than a bribe held out
to somebody to wish the party insured dead. Hence a policy
on a life can only be issued for the benefit of some person
who would lose at least as much by the death of the insured
as the amount of the policy. The life of a debtor may properly be insured for the benefit of the creditor to the amount
of the debt. But the life of a creditor cannot be insured for
the benefit of the debtor to any amount. The life of the husband may be insured for the benefit of the wife, if his death
would involve a loss of pecuniary support to her. Otherwise
not. If the death of the wife involves no pecuniary loss to
the husband, either a policy on her life for his benefit, or a
joint policy on the two lives for the benefit of the survivor, is
essentially vicious. Yet policies of this sort are quite too
often issued. Policies are seldom issued on lives advanced
beyond the age of sixty-five. On our registry is not one entered at an age so advanced as eighty, yet more than 100 beyond seventy-five are insured by policies issued earlier. Now

it there is any reason why a policy should not be issued on a life older than seventy-five, there is the same, if not more, reason why no policy issued at an earlier age should cover a period beyond seventy-five. For the only reason to justify issuing a policy at seventy-five, would be the existence somewhere of an insurable interest in the life, and the fact of its existence could be better known at that age than at any previous one. Hence the companies cannot justify themselves in refusing to issue policies at an advanced age without equally condemning themselves for issuing at earlier ages policies to extend beyond that age.

A simple analysis of a whole-life policy of insurance demonstrates its impropriety. Suppose the policy taken at the age of thirty for one thousand dollars, at a premium paid down at once of $409.51, or of $22.70 paid annually during life. Practically, the single premium is high and the annual premium low, but they are exactly equivalent, the one to the other, so far as the company is concerned, on the assumption that interest will always be four per cent. and the mortality that of the actuaries' rate. It does not follow from this that they are the same to the insured, the same assumptions being true. As the rate of mortality is graduated by years, and interest is paid annually, the contract between the company and the insured party, whether the premium be single or annual, necessarily resolves itself into as many separate and distinct bets as the assured has possible years of life before him. The Actuaries' Rate of Mortality assumes—for the purpose of calculation—that it is impossible for any person to live beyond the age of 100 years. Whether this be true or not, it is near enough to the truth for the purpose. Hence in any whole-life policy entered at the age of thirty, there are precisely seventy distinct and separate bets, and, under the scale of mortality assumed, it cannot be regarded otherwise without utter confusion.* In regard to each and every possible year

* That is, if the distinction between insurance and self-insurance is not recognized.

of his future life, the company bets that the insured party will *not* die in it; and in regard to each and every such year, the insured party bets that he *will* die in it. In the case of a single premium, the party insured deposits with the company—which always holds the stakes—the stakes on his seventy bets all at once; for example, on the bet that he will die in his thirty-first year of age, $10.83; on the bet that he will die in his thirty-second year, $10.48; on the bet that he will die in his sixty-first year, $7.78; on the bet that he will die in his eighty-first year, $3.90; on the bet that he will die in his ninety-first year, sixty cents; and on the bet that he will die in his 100th year, *one mill*, nearly. The aggregate of these seventy small stakes is $409.51. But if the annual premium of $22.70 is paid, then the full stake on the first of the seventy bets is paid the first year, to wit: $10.83, the same as in the other case, and the remaining $11.87 is deposited, not on the next one or two, but on all the remaining sixty-nine bets, in proportion to the present value of the risk of $1,000 on each. That is, thirty-one cents is deposited on the bet that the party will die in his thirty-second year; twenty-three cents on the bet that he will die in his sixty-first year; twelve cents that he will die in his eighty-first year; four cents that he will die in his ninety-first year, and about three per cent. of one mill that he will die in his 100th year. If he survives to pay the second annual premium, he in fact deposits on each of the sixty-nine remaining bets, completing the stake on the first, and adding something to each of the others. Now, the point to which we wish to call attention is, that these bets are all perfectly distinct and independent. In regard to the first year, the bet is justified by the known existence of an insurable interest in the life which is the subject of it. The succeeding bets may be justified by the probability of the continuance of such insurable interest, and by the fact that unless contracted while the party is in sound health, they cannot be contracted at all. But the justification depends upon and is proportional to the probability aforesaid, and entirely fades out with it. Now the probability of the existence of an insurable interest at the age of sixty may be sufficient to justify nailing the bet by the deposit of twenty-three cents, or even by paying $7.78, the full stake; but what can justify staking $3.90, or any money whatever, on the bet in regard to the eighty-first year of life, when there is no reasonable probability of insurable interest? It is gambling of the worst kind, and all that can be said in its favor is, that it sticks like a barnacle to a kind which is useful, and safe only because it is useful.

We should shrink with horror from applying life insurance to infants, though the hopes that cluster around them may easily be conceived to have a money value. Why, then, do we insure second childhood, in which hope will have given place to history? The only use of insurance betting is to guard-against the pecuniary or financial evil of the sudden cessation of productive energy or capital. To bet money in order to secure a money indemnity for the loss of a life that produces no money, is worse than buying tickets in a lottery, or staking money on the turn of dice.

We remarked, in giving the foregoing analysis of a whole-life policy, that it was the same thing to the company whether it was paid by a single or an annual premium, certain assumptions being true, but not the same to the insured. It would be the same to that practical impossibility, a mathematically average policy-holder, or to one as rich as the company; but it is just because a man is nothing of the sort that he seeks to be insured. It is because he wants to provide against the first half of the chances of death more than against the last, that he takes a policy. If he takes a whole-life policy at thirty, he is sure to lose sixty-nine of his seventy bets, and win on one. As an average matter, or taking one case with another in thousands, it will make no difference to him whether the stakes are all paid at the first, or only made np as fant as the bets are to determine. The average man pays the same in either case. But if the insured party wins the first bet, by dying in the first year, he loses only what he has deposited on the others, that is, $11.87 if he has paid the annual premium, and $398.68 if he has paid the single premium. This paying single premiums, it will be perceived, is taking the game butt end foremost, and going at it as if you were yourself a gambling bank or an insurance office. Or taking another view of it, it is purchasing of the company an annuity on your life to pay all the premiums but the first. And if the insurance is a good investment for you, for the very same reason the annuity—which is the largest part of the transaction—is a bad one, and *vice versa.*

Whoever has faithfully waded through these long extracts, will not fail to have perceived that the writer's mind, though seeing some things, was in a dense muddle from using the old-fashioned spectacles, which resolve the whole business into bets, for better or worse. Admitting the truth of this view, and it is undeniably the theory on which the practice had proceeded, it was obvious enough on what principles the undetermined bets must be cancelled, if cancelled equitably. Indeed, it was so obvious, that the president of that company which had always cancelled the least equitably, and on that account had made the largest dividends, immediately on the publication of that report addressed to its author an earnest remonstrance against illustrating life insurance by the science of betting, contending that its accumulation ought always to be regarded and spoken of as deposits in a savings bank. There was good reason in this, if anybody had ever only looked at the subject right end foremost. Unfortunately that letter has been lost or it would be printed in this connection. The writer of it has been taken at his word, but he still sticks to the *practice* founded on the theory, that the *whole* business is betting, ignores *self-insurance*, and insists on making "savings bank" as applied to life insurance a misnomer and a sham.

Chapter III.

SURRENDER CHARGE.

For the best life a *minimum* premium is stipulated, and this is never diminished, except by return of demonstrated surplus. Can there be a *maximum* charge to be paid *equitably* by the best life in case of the surrender of the policy at any subsequent time? Can this be stipulated in the policy as well as the payment of the whole face of the policy either at death or survival of the term? These questions, essentially mathematical, were brought before the mathematical advisers of the life insurance companies of this country three years ago, as will be seen on a subsequent page. [See letter to Mr. White.] Instead of a convention of the executive officers of these companies to settle them, at the instance of the largest and most auto-

cratically governed company, a convention of State
insurance superintendents was called by George
W. Miller, the lately discarded superintendent of
the Insurance Department of New York, apparently
for the very purpose, among others equally injuri-
ous to policy-holders and the public, of preventing
a fair and equitable settlement of them. This officer
who was president as well as caller of that remarkable convention, which had two costly sessions at
the expense of the policy-holders, has since been
publicly convicted of being the overpaid tool of
parties who prey upon the policy-holder. How he
served the life-insurance autocracies, while he was
in power, the reports of this wonderful convention
fully show. It is their aim always to get into their
hands and retain as much of other people's money
as they can, without regard to justice or equity,
and they used this convention, so finely headed, to
throw an immense fog-bank over the eyes of the
people, in the form of scientific research, on these
very questions. It was in the report of the first
session of this convention that the lucubrations of
the present actuary of the Mutual Life, Professor
Bartlett, formerly of West Point,—the promise of
which by Judge McCurdy had defeated in the
Massachusetts Senate the bill on page 52—first saw
the light, so far as the present writer is informed.

In this remarkable paper, the distinguished professor comes to the point of " surrender charge " in

the following paragraphs. [See First Session, Offi-cial Report of National Insurance Convention. J. H. and C. M. Goodsell, New York, 1871, page 141.]

" It would relieve the question of much embarrassment, if medical advisers could designate, with any tolerable precis-ion, the number of years an applicant for surrender would probably live. But as this cannot be, the mathematician must solve the problem on the assumption that the only differences of vital powers are those arising from differences of ages. The results of the solution made upon this hypothe-sis, should, however, be modified in amount and made to conform somewhat to the judgment of medical counsel and officers of the company.

" Supposing, then, that the members of a company are equally good in all respects, except in the matter of age, the determination of the surrender value will result from the fact that the company and each of its members have a joint inter-est in the policy of the latter. The present values of these interests being found, their difference, it is clear, will be the value sought.

" 1. What is the company's interest in any particular policy? Obviously, the present value of the sums the policy would, if continued in the company in its present condition, contribute from year to year, to pay death claims on other policies.

" 2. What is the interest of the assured or of his heirs in his policy? The answer is, the present value of the reversion or sum the latter would receive at death of the owner, pro-vided he pay nothing more than he has already paid. This is, obviously, the present reserve."

The significance of the " insurance value " of a policy or what it may be expected to contribute to

the death-claims of the company over and above
what it will contribute by "*self-insurance,*" or
accumulation, to its own, having then been discovered and recognized for more than a year, a
person so scientific as the distinguished West Point
Professor could not in treating of this subject leave
it out of the account, even out of deference to the
wishes and interests of the autocratic manager of
millions.   But in the drollest way, for a mathematical man, he does leave out of the account
entirely, *the interest of the policy-holder in the
insurance to be done by the company*, which in the
case he supposes, of an average life, is precisely
the "insurance value," or equal to the interest of
the company in him.   In other words, the retiring
member with a vitality no better or worse than the
average in getting released from further payment of
net premiums, releases the company from an obligation to insure him further, of exactly the same
value.   And in getting himself released from paying any further loading or provision for expenses
he releases the company from the necessity of
spending anything further on his account.   Consequently in the case supposed by the Professor there
is really, in a purely Mutual Company, no ground
for any "surrender charge" or deduction from the
"self-insurance" fund, whatever.   It is only when
the life is *better* than the average, that the company's interest in the insurance to be surrendered

exceeds the value of the obligation to insure from which it is released. And what it has an equitable right to deduct from the self-insurance or private accumulation of the applicant for surrender, is not by any means what an average life may be expected to contribute "to death-claims on other policies" but what this life may be expected to contribute over and above an average one. This, though it is not the "insurance value," and cannot well be supposed ever to be equal to it, will undoubtedly bear some ratio to it.

The paper of Prof. Bartlett after thus deciding the great question, proceeds to an algebraic demonstration, or rather expression, of his views, in which what was true could not be new at that date. This having been rather mercilessly criticised in the "Insurance Times" by a much younger mathematician, Prof. Bartlett addressed a letter to Gen. Gustavus W. Smith of the Convention, in which he gives his algebra in a revised form, and distinctly recedes from the absurd position of making the *whole* insurance value the surrender charge in case of an ordinary life policy, though he clings to the equal absurdity, though smaller enormity, of making it so in the case of a "paid up" or single premium policy.

This letter, which may be supposed to contain Professor Bartlett's fully matured view of the question, with the writer's reply to it in the N. Y.

"Insurance Times," of September, 1872, are given in full in the following pages. The general reader will not fail to grasp the pith of the matter, though he should get no light from the algebra, which he will be kind enough to excuse on account of the great amusement it will cause to the technical reader.

NEW YORK, September 13, 1871.

General G. W. SMITH, *Insurance Commissioner of Kentucky, Chairman, etc., etc.*

DEAR SIR:—Numerous inquiries, made verbally and by letter, indicate that the mathematical work in my letter to you of last June, on the subject of surrender value, is not understood, and the object of this is to clear up whatever of doubt there may be about its meaning. When that letter was written, I did not suppose its mathematics would be published. It was very condensed; but, knowing your habit of scrutinizing everything brought under the exercise of your judgment, I felt that whatever of obscurity, if any, there might be about it, could and would be dispelled by an interchange of ideas between us.

I will not repeat the prefatory remarks by which the work was introduced, but that you may the more fully appreciate the spirit in which it was undertaken, it may be proper to say, that I have never been able to regard the institution of life assurance as a mere business concern, of which the main object is to make money. It has always appeared to me rather as a fraternal charity, created by the voluntary union of persons for mutual protection against the calamities of sudden penury to helpless widows and orphans—always dispensing the largest liberality towards its members, consistent with equal justice to all. Of course, this view shuts out all consideration of what is known as the "joint stock interest."

All persons having any acquaintance with principles of permutation and combination of elements, must know that the variety of policies a company may issue is very great. I shall confine myself now, as before, to the more popular and common cases.

LIFE.—SINGLE PREMIUM.

The premium paid on this kind of policy, resolves itself, in effect, into two portions, one of which, with its interest accumulations, constitutes the policy-holders' share of the annual death-claims, and to the end of what may be called his tabular life; and the other works at compound interest till it amounts, at the same epoch, to the sum assured. Those who die early leave to their heirs more than they contribute to the company, and those who die late leave their heirs less. A company, therefore naturally covets a longevity amongst its members, greater than the average duration of human life.

It will be conceded that the retiring of members works damage to a company's vital force. Indeed, it is easy to conceive that the process may be conducted in a way and carried to an extent which would turn the advantages of selection against a company. In the case of paid-up life policies, the rule that only good lives surrender, may be regarded as almost certain. They have nothing more to pay, and retire because of confidence in a superior physical condition and a belief that they can do better with their money. The settlement with these should be so made as to provide against the adverse effects to the company, likely to arise from their own voluntary act. They should be retired under conditions that would leave the relation between the present financial resources of the company and its future obligations, as affected by the considerations above stated, undisturbed. These conditions may be fulfilled by giving to a retiring

4

member, the money working to reach the sum assured, which
must sooner or later pass by death to his heirs, and retaining
that pledged for future death-claims.

The sum of these constitutes, at any instant, the assured's
reserve. The difference between the reserve and that appro-
priated to death-claims, is, it seems to me, an equitable surrender value. To compute it, make—

$\Pi_x=$.Single net premium at age x, to assure one dollar at
death.

$R_x=$.Net reserve at age x, on a dollar paid-up policy.

$m=$.Number of years a policy has to run to maturity.

$n=$.Difference between the oldest age of the tables and that
of policy-holder at time of surrender;

$S=$.Sum assured;

$Q=$.Surrender value,

$T_x=C_x.R_x+1+C_x+1.R^x+2+\quad\ldots\quad C_{x+n}.R_{x+n}+1$, in which
$R_{x+n}+1=0$.

Then $Q=S.\dfrac{T_x}{D_x}$ . . . . . (1)

The following examples will exhibit the results of the rule
by the American table and four per cent. on single premium
policies for $1,000, at a few ages :—

Age, 40,	.	.	.	$227.889	Age, 91,	.	.	$889.826
50,	.	.	.	318.134	92,	.	.	903.281
60,	.	.	.	437.895	93,	.	.	921.276
70,	.	.	.	580.167	94,	.	.	936.040
80,	.	.	.	729.236	95,	.	.	961.538
90,	.	.	.	875.803	96,	.	.	1,000.000

LIFE.—ANNUAL PREMIUMS.

Members who engage to pay annual premiums for life, or
for a limited term, more frequently retire because of a want
of means to keep their premium engagements; the company is not likely to suffer so much from adverse selection,

the question is narrowed down to forfeiture or sale, and it can, therefore, exercise a greater liberality with safety to itself. I treat the reserves on these policies exactly as though they had come from a paid-up policy, but not for the purpose of exchange. Let R'_x, be the reserve on an annual premium policy for one dollar. Another policy taken out by the same holder, at the same time, but paid up and for an amount that would have the same reserve, R'_x, at the time of surrender, would have for its reversionary value

and the surrender $$S.\frac{R'_x}{R_x}=S.\frac{R'_x}{\Pi_x};$$

$$Q=S.\frac{R'_x.T_x}{R_x D_x}=S.\frac{R'_x.T_x}{\Pi_x D_x} \quad \cdots \cdots \quad (2)$$

Now, this conversion of an annual premium-paying policy into an auxiliary paid-up one, is not for the purpose, as above stated, of exchange, but to secure the equities of an actual surrender, to shorten labor and save time and expense in settling with a retiring member.

The following example of a policy for $1,000, issued at age 35, and surrendered at various ages to the end of life, will illustrate the rule.

AGE.				Surrender Value.	AGE.				Surrender Value.
36,	.	.	.	.	$6 38	50,	.	.	.	.	$140 25
37,	.	.	.	.	13 14	51,	.	.	.	.	153 23
38,	.	.	.	.	20 29	52,	.	.	.	.	166 66
39,	.	.	.	.	27 84	53,	.	.	.	.	180 54
40,	.	.	.	.	35 81	54,	.	.	.	.	194 84
41,	.	.	.	.	44 20	55,	.	.	.	.	209 57
42,	.	.	.	.	53 03	56,	.	.	.	.	224 71
43,	.	.	.	.	62 30	57,	.	.	.	.	240 24
44,	.	.	.	.	72 04	58,	.	.	.	.	256 16
45,	.	.	.	.	82 23	59,	.	.	.	.	272 46
46,	.	.	.	.	92 90	60,	.	.	.	.	289 10
47,	.	.	.	.	104 03	61,	.	.	.	.	306 07
48,	.	.	.	.	115 64	62,	.	.	.	.	323 34
49,	.	.	.	.	127 72	63.	.	.	.	.	340 89

AGE.				Surrender Value.	AGE.				Surrender Value.
64,	.	.	.	.	$358 71	81,	.	.	.	.	$675 79
65,	.	.	.	.	376 74	82,	.	.	.	.	694 92
66,	.	.	.	.	394 96	83,	.	.	.	.	713 66
67,	.	.	.	.	413 34	84,	.	.	.	.	732 68
68,	.	.	.	.	431 84	85,	.	.	.	.	751 79
69,	.	.	.	.	450 42	86,	.	.	.	.	770 83
70,	.	.	.	.	469 04	87,	.	.	.	.	789 54
71,	.	.	.	.	487 68	88,	.	.	.	.	807 64
72,	.	.	.	.	506 31	89,	.	.	.	.	825 26
73,	.	.	.	.	524 93	90,	.	.	.	.	842 13
74,	.	.	.	.	543 58	91,	.	.	.	.	859 77
75,	.	.	.	.	562 27	92,	.	.	.	.	877 77
76,	.	.	.	.	581 03	93,	.	.	.	.	896 25
77,	.	.	.	.	599 88	94,	.	.	.	.	903 77
78,	.	.	.	.	618 81	95,	.	.	.	.	942 69
79,	.	.	.	.	637 79	96,	.	.	.	.	1,000 00
80,	.	.	.	.	656 82					

LIFE.—LIMITED PAYMENTS.

For reasons stated

$$\mathcal{Q} = S \cdot \frac{R'_x}{\Pi_x} \cdot \frac{T_x}{D_x}. \qquad \qquad \text{(4)}$$

TEMPORARY.—SINGLE PAYMENT.

Here

$$\mathcal{Q} = S \cdot \frac{C_x \cdot R_x + 1 + C_x + 1 R_x + 2 \quad \dots \quad + C_x + m + 2 R_x + m - 1}{D_x}$$

or

$$\mathcal{Q} = S \cdot \frac{C_x \cdot R_x + 1, \overline{m-1}}{D_x} \qquad \qquad \text{(5)}$$

TEMPORARY.—ANNUAL PAYMENTS.

Take the Reserve R'$_x$, as having arisen from a paid-up policy of which the reversionary amount is determined, as before, and we get

$$\mathcal{Q} = S \cdot \frac{R'_x}{\pi'_x} \cdot \frac{C_x \cdot R_x + 1, \overline{m-1}}{D_x} \qquad \qquad \text{(6)}$$

SIMPLE ENDOWMENTS.—SINGLE PREMIUMS.

The company has no interest in the longevity of the holders of this kind of policy,—on the contrary, by the principle of the Tontine, its interest is in their early death, at least death before maturity.

The reserve on this kind of policy being $\overline{R_x}$, there are l_x, chances for and against the company: of these $d_x + d_{x+1} + \ldots \quad d_{x+m-1}$, favor lapse by death; and the surrender value is given by

$$\overline{\mathcal{Q}} = S . R_x \left(1 - \frac{d_x + d_{x+1} + \quad \ldots \quad d_{x+m-1}}{l_x} ; \right)$$

$$\overline{\mathcal{Q}} = S . \overline{R_x} . \frac{l_{x+m}}{l_x} . \quad \ldots \quad (7)$$

SIMPLE ENDOWMENTS.—ANNUAL PREMIUM.

The reserve on this being $\overline{R'_x}$,

$$\overline{\mathcal{Q}} = S . \overline{R'_x} . \frac{l_{x+m}}{l_x} \quad \ldots \quad (8)$$

ENDOWMENT ASSURANCES.—SINGLE PREMIUM.

Take sum of equations (5) and (7)

$$\mathcal{Q} + \overline{\mathcal{Q}} = S . \left[\frac{C_x . R_{x+1} \overline{m-1}}{. D_x} + R_x . \frac{l_{x+m}}{l_x} \right] \quad \ldots \quad (9)$$

ENDOWMENT ASSURANCES.—ANNUAL PREMIUM.

Take sum of equations (6) and (8)

$$\mathcal{Q} + \mathcal{Q} = S . \left[\frac{R'_x}{\pi'_x} . \frac{C_x . R_{x+1, \overline{m-1}}}{D_x} + R'_x . \frac{l_{x+m}}{l_x} \right] \quad \ldots \quad (10)$$

The first terms in the brackets of equations (9) and (10), become very small for short term policies and for small amounts, and may be neglected without much error.

The following example of a ten-year endowment assurance, issued at age 35, for $1,000, will illustrate:—

A G E.	Surrender Value.	A G E.	Surrender Value.
36, ...	$72.486	41, ...	$516.974
37, ...	149.921	42, ...	625.979
38, ...	232.673	43, ...	741.553
39, ...	321.130	44, ...	866.167
40, ...	415.736	45, ...	1,000.000

Such is my solution of the question of surrender value for the more popular and common policies, in so far as the elements that pertain to this complex problem have been subjected to mathematical analysis by myself. I like it, and it suits me better than anything of the kind I have yet seen. It gives surrender values more equitable and considerably greater than companies have been in the habit of paying.

Permit me, in closing this letter, to express the hope that the labors of yourself and your colleagues in the convention, may result in greater uniformity in the insurance laws of the different states, and in the dissemination of knowledge on this and kindred subjects, which shall prevent unwise and unfriendly legislation.

Very truly yours,

WM. H. C. BARTLETT.

[From the Insurance Times, September, 1872.]

SURRENDER CHARGE.

" The present value of the sums the policy would contribute from year to year, if continued in the company in its present condition, to pay death-claims on other policies, will pay in advance for all the insurance the policy-holder will get from the company if he remains in it, because it pays for insurance on the amount the company has at risk from year to year, and the policy-holder's own money on deposit makes up the balance of the policy. *With the light before us, we have utterly failed to see that this has any relation to the surrender charge a company should make in case a policy-holder withdraws.* When the actuaries agree amongst themselves on this point, the subject will merit, and will probably receive further consideration at the hands of those most interested,—the policy-holders and the companies." —*Report of the National Insurance Convention, second session, Appendix, page* 75.

The italics in the quotation above are mine, and intended to express some surprise that such a sentence should follow that which precedes it. If the Superintendents cannot see that there is any relation between the amount of the insurance business withdrawn by a policy-holder, in cancelling his contract and the charge the company should make against him for withdrawing, there seems little use in discussing with them what that relation should be. Supposing the policy-holder and the company were equally desirous of cancelling the contract, the policy-holder as much wishing to be released from further payments, as the company from carrying the risk further, there should be no charge at all. But if the policy-holder alone desires to be released, and the company considering that the future payments will more than compensate for the future risks, wishes to retain the policy, it seems necessary and inevitable that the advantage to the company of retaining the policy must bear some relation to the present value of the future payments. Of course it could not equal it, for that would be to suppose no risk of dying. The charge should, if possible, be equal to the advantage surrendered. This advantage is a certain portion of the normal costs of carrying the future risks. Other things being equal, it cannot but be proportional to the present value of those costs when we compare two policies.

But utterly as the Superintendents have failed to see this relation, or any other by which the proper charge for the

surrender of a policy can be determined, they admit that
when the actuaries agree among themselves on this point,
the subject will merit and receive the attention of the policy-
holders and the companies. I respectfully submit that it
deserves their attention the more, if the actuaries do not
agree. The more the doctors differ, the more it behooves
the patients to look out for themselves.

Judging from the expressed opinions of the actuaries referred to in this Report of the National Insurance Convention, they do agree in seeing *some* relation between surrender
charge and insurance value. They only differ as to how this
relation shall be applied, or perhaps, as to whether the charge
should have any relation to anything else.

Now it is quite possible that by a diligent study of these
opinions, and the reasons expressed to sustain them, the
policy-holders and the companies may be able to satisfy
themselves which of the actuaries is correct. It is with a
view of aiding in this study that I refer to Professor Bartlett's
elaborate paper on this subject, printed in this " National Insurance Report," pages 6–10.

In regard to a single premium life policy, the distinguished
actuary of the Mutual Life distinctly admits that the proper
surrender charge has a relation to the insurance value of the
policy at the time of surrender, and to nothing else. But for
reasons which he does not very distinctly state, and which are
very far from being apparent, he fixes the charge at precisely
one hundred per cent. of the insurance value. That is to say,
he would give the retiring member his self-insurance, " the
money working to reach the sum assured," and retain the
whole of that sum which is working to pay for the insurance
he will receive during that process. It certainly cannot be
said that this is an *unsafe* proceeding for the company, for it
exacts, in regard to the future insurance, full payment and
carries no risk! The handle of this jug is entirely on one
side. The retiring member, for the sake of getting back his

own deposit, not a dollar of which could ever be used to pay any death-claim besides his own, pays the company not merely what profit it might expect to make by insuring him, but the whole cost of insuring him, supposing him to be a risk on which no profit could be made. This is exactly as if B should hire a horse of A for a week, agreeing to pay $30 for its use, and depositing with A as security a bond for $100. After a day's use, he offers to surrender the horse, pay $5 for one day's use, and the damage to A by the loss of profit on the other five days. "No," says A, adopting the logic of Professor Bartlett, "surrender the horse, and pay me the other $25 also, and the bond is yours." Even this on the part of the livery-stable man would be liberal compared with what *some* life-insurance men have been known to do.

Let me illustrate by one of Professor Bartlett's own examples. Using the "American Experience," at four per cent., the reserve on a paid-up policy for $1,000 is $367.58. Of this, $139.69 is the insurance value, or the sum which, accumulating at four per cent., will be sufficient to pay for all the yearly risks to be borne by the company. These risks, it is to be remembered, are a series beginning with the complement of the reserve for the next year and gradually diminishing to nothing at the last. The residue of $227.89 is accumulating at the same rate of interest, so as to make, in addition to the sum insured by the company, exactly $1,000 at the end of any year in which the death may occur. This $227.89 is therefore a mere deposit, the whole function of which is to limit the company's risk till it ceases at 95. There is no possible profit to be made out of it by the company, and therefore, if the policy-holder retires, Professor Bartlett very properly admits that he may withdraw the whole of it. But although it is clear enough that if he withdraws he will not enjoy another particle of the insurance for which he has paid $139.69, Professor Bartlett insists that he shall leave the *whole* of that with the company. Where is the equity of making

4*

people pay as much for nothing as for something? If it costs
something to carry even the lightest risks, it must be worth
something to be released from carrying them, and this something, whatever it may fairly be supposed to be, should be
deducted from the $139.69 and given to the retiring member,
in addition to his deposit of $227.89, and only the remainder
should be retained by the company as a snrrender charge.

The quality of Prof. Bartlett's "equities of an actual surrender" becomes still more apparent when he proposes to apply
them to a paid-up term policy. Here his abbreviated formula
to express the surrender value, Q, of a policy for a unit to
run m years is,

$$Q = \frac{C_x R_{x+1, \overline{m-1}}}{D_x}$$

Putting $x=36$ and $m=9$ we have by American Experience
4 per cent.

$$Q = \frac{C_{36} R_{37, \overline{8}}}{D_{36}} = .0025706.$$

Hence the surrender value for $1,000 is $2.57, while the reserve is $70.26, making the charge $67.69. This latter sum
would pay for all the insurance to be done by the company
in nine years. If the $2.57, which was sufficient to provide
for the small self-insurance on such a policy, is all that the
retiring member has taken away on releasing the company
from its obligations, he is likely to carry with him more awe·
for the mysteries of life insurance than admiration of its
science or respect for its justice.

There is not much term insurance in existence, and very
little of that is paid up. And there are still fewer pure endowment policies of any sort, so that the value of surrender
for these two classes of policies is comparatively of little
practical importance. But the most desirable and popular
policies arc those which may be regarded as combining term
insurance with pure endowment, though for business purposes

it is far more convenient to regard them as combining a series of diminishing insurances with a series of annual trust or savings-bank deposits, and to eliminate altogether the element of chance from the endowment part of the business, making it, in fact, self-endowment instead of tontine. For such policies a better rule of surrender than has thus far been much practised is a vital necessity. Towards such a rule Prof. Bartlett would have taken a long stride if, when he came to consider the paid-up pure endowment, he had not deserted his principle of making the insurance value the surrender charge. If he had stuck to that, his abbreviated formula (7) page 9, for the value of Q for a unit of policy, would have been

$$Q = \frac{C_x R_{x+1, \overline{m-1}} + v D_{x+m-1}}{D_x}$$

which, putting $x=36$ and $m=9$, as before, would give $SQ = 700.24$, if I do not mistake the figures. The reason why this surrender value exceeds the reserve, which is only $642.65, is that the insurance value of this policy is necessarily negative. The application of the principle here would of course be as frightful to the company, as in the other case it was to the retiring member, but it is mathematically as good in this case as in the other, the hypopthesis being that the retiring life is better than the average, which implies that the company can well afford to pay something to get rid of it.

But since in the case of pure endowment it is the worst lives that are most tempted to retire, and it is for the interest of the company to have them remain, it is very proper for the actuary, who is paid by the company and not by the retiring members, to propose a different principle of surrender in this case. By the contract the company has agreed, we will say, to pay $1,000 to a party on his reaching the age of 45, and as a fair consideration for his chance of receiving it he has paid a sum which, at his present age of 36, has become $642.65, the whole of which and its interest he is to lose if he dies under 45. On the hypothesis that money is worth 4 per cent., and the life is an average one, the company has nothing to gain or lose by the contract, and of course the equitable surrender value is precisely \$642.65. But the company will gain by the continuance of the policy if the life is worse than the average, and Prof. Bartlett, on this hypothesis apparently, proposes, as a penalty for retirement, to deduct \$54.82 from \$642.65, and return \$587.83.

In general terms he proposes to find $\overline{Q}$, the surrender value of a unit of paid-up endowment, by the formula (7.) :

$$\overline{Q} = \overline{R}_x \frac{l_{x+m}}{l_x} \qquad •$$

For the particular purpose of guarding against the loss of profitable pure endowment policies this is no more objectionable than charging the whole insurance value on insurance policies, and, indeed, not quite so much so. And there is much ingenuity in getting rid of the negative sign.* But the

---

* Professor Bartlett's surrender charge in this case is for a unit of policy,

$$\overline{R}_x - R_x \frac{l_{x+m}}{l_x}$$

which differs from the insurance value, or present value of the *negative* normal costs of insurance, not only in being positive, but in being necessarily a little smaller than

$$\frac{C_x \overline{R}_{x+1}, \overline{m-1} + vD_{x+m-1}}{D_x} \overline{R}_x$$

which expresses the insurance value; because, while he discounts $r^m R_x$ by both mortality and interest, from age $x+m$ to x, into

$$R_x \frac{l_{x+m}}{l_x}$$

he also discounts in the same way $1 - r^m R_x$, the accumulated yearly tontine profits (properly enough assumed to be positive for the purpose above referred to) at age $x+m$ into

Professor does not leave it for this particular use, which is rather imaginary than real. He comes down upon paid-up endowment insurance with it, and is thus enabled to cut a mathematical antic which is truly marvellous. He adds the surrender value of the paid-up term policy, found on the hypothesis that the life is better than the average, to the surrender value of the paid-up endowment for the same term, found on the contrary hypothesis that it is worse, and thus finds the surrender value of the combined paid-up endowment insurance policy! Thus combining the two policies above cited, they have a reserve at 36 of $712.91. Adding the two surrender values, $2.57+$587.83=$590.40, we have made a charge of $67.69+$54.82=$122.51, or more than ten times the whole insurance value of the combined endowment insurance policy. The adding of the surrender values is a perfectly correct proceeding, and if the professor had not deserted his principle in treating the pure endowment, the surrender charge for the endowment insurance would have been exactly its insurance value, or $10.10.

As in this combined policy the endowment bet never fully

$$v^m \frac{l_{x+m}}{l_x} - R_1 \frac{l_{x+m}}{l_x} = R_2 - R_2 \frac{l_{x+m}}{x\,l_x}$$

manifestly a smaller result than if he had discounted the amount at age $x+m$ of each yearly tontine profit, from age $x+m$ to the date of its development by the rate of interest only, and from that date to age x by both mortality and interest, and taken the aggregate.

And here I wish to express my regret, as I have had occasion to for such blunders often before, that on recurring to my own formula for the insurance value of a paid-up pure endowment in the preface to the revised edition of my 4 per cent. Valuation Tables (page 7, equation nearest the bottom), I notice an unaccountable error in the omission of a positive term in the second member of the equation, which, however, any algebraist will readily supply by subtracting the equation for the insurance value of a paid-up term policy from that for the insurance value of a paid-up endowment insurance for the same term, as given in the remarks that precede the error.

hedges the insurance bet, except in the last year, and as the
same life cannot be both better and worse than the average at
the same time, the more reasonable assumption for the company to make, in case a surrender of one of these policies is
called for, is that the life is better than the average. If so,
the company loses by the surrender of the term policy and
gains by that of the endowment, in proportion to the insurance
value of each. That is to say, if it is equitable to charge the
retiring member as Prof. Bartlett proposes to do, $67.69 for
the surrender of the term policy, it must be equally so to
credit him $57.59 for the surrender of the endowment. He
will then pay full price for all the future insurance on the
policy without getting it, which is certainly ten times too much,
unless it can be proved in some way that trustees have a
right to charge for their services more than the interest of
money entrusted to them.

Notwithstanding the palpable want of equity or fairness in
charging the whole insurance value for surrender in any
case, Prof. Bartlett's plan is, on the whole, a considerable
improvement upon what has been usually practised of charging one-half or one-third, if not the whole of the reserve, for
in regard to annual premium policies offering to surrender,
in which case his rule would work the most onerously to the
retiring member, it is not the insurance value of the policy to
be surrendered which he charges, but that of an imaginary
paid-up policy with the same reserve. By this substitution of
a vicarious policy for the real one, without much regard to
the question whether the company could afford to give such
a policy or not, it comes about that the surrender charge on
an ordinary life policy of annual premiums is made to vary
from two or three per cent. of its insurance value, which is
quite too small, to a little more than fifty per cent, which is
much too large—but not so bad, I cheerfully admit, as one
hundred per cent. would be. It seldom runs much above
thirty per cent. of the reserve, which is an obvious improve-

ment upon fifty per cent. when the reserve is large. It is easy, by comparing almost any two examples to see the practical arbitrariness òf the rule. These will suffice.

A is a life policy for \$1,000, entered at 35, which has paid fifteen annual premiums. B another of the same amount on the same life, entered at 49. Their respective reserves, insurance values, surrender charges and surrender values, according to Professor Bartlett's formulas, are as follows:

	Reserve.	Ins. Value.	Sur. Charge.	Sur. Value.
A, . . .	\$205 87	\$221 80	\$65 62	\$140 25
B, . . .	22 23	273 55	7 26	14 97

· For A the charge is 29.58 per cent. of its insurance value; for B it is but 2.65 per cent. Both of these charges cannot be correct unless the surrender charge is to be regulated by some other relation than that to insurance value. It obviously comes much nearer being proportionate to the reserve, but the reserve is no measure of the company's loss of strength in losing the policy. In one case the charge is sufficient to pay an agent nearly the two first premiums for getting another policy as valuable as the one surrendered. In the other case it is only sufficient to pay about half the usual commission. Is this business-like?

When Prof. Bartlett comes to apply his double-action rule of surrender charge to endowment insurance policies of annual premiums—a class of policies for which an equitable value is particularly needed—the arbitrariness of making the same game venison for one purpose and veal for another, is still more striking. Here is policy A, a ten-year endowment insurance for \$1,000, taken at age 35, which has paid eight premiums, and B a policy for the same amount and term, on the same life, taken at 42. The reserves, insurance values, surrender charges and surrender values, according to Prof. Bartlett's formulas, as near as I can get the figures with extemporaneous tables, are:

	Reserve.	Ins. Value.	Sur. Charge.	Sur. Value.
A, . . .	$759 44	$1 31	$17 89	$741 55
B, . . .	79 68	38 91	9 77	69 91

Behold a rule by which for the same life a company charges $8.12 more for the surrender of a policy which is worth $37.60 less! Is this the way "to secure the equities of an actual surrender"?

Now when policies are being surrendered at the rate of some $300,000,000 a year, or about as fast as they can be acquired, and the retiring members pervade the community with more or less vocal expression of dissatisfied minds—when the Mutual Life itself pays more than a million of dollars a year as surrender value—does it not seem time that the executive officers of the companies should agree upon some rule of surrender charge which the policyholders can understand and appreciate, and which will keep the companies from decaying as fast or faster than they grow, whether the actuaries can agree to it or not?

As a sequel and clincher to this discussion on surrender charge, the writer published in the "Insurance Times" of December, 1872, the following question, which nobody, thus far, seems to have answered.

A Conundrum on Life Insurance.

The question to be propounded in this article interests more or less not only every existing policy-holder, but every future, or possible one. Those who are at all sensitive about such interest had better watch carefully for the answer. Lest it should be slow in coming, they are advised to cut out the conundrum bodily with a pair of scissors, and put it directly to every life-insurance agent, president, actuary, editor, or man of figures they meet. It will not be best to bother the British Institute of Actuaries with it, for the life-insurance companies which nestle most securely under the wings of that profoundly scientific body do not say much about paying surrender value, equitable or otherwise. On the contrary, if a policy-holder there wishes to retire and cease paying premiums, he seems to have no other means of recovering any part of his self-insurance from any respectable office in London, than to sell his policy to some outside speculator, who, without a particle of insurable interest in the life, pays the premiums in the hope of an early, and to him lucky, death, when he receives the whole face of the policy.

In this country our life-insurance companies have not been so scientific as to open this charming vista for predestined octogenarians. Take up the prospectus or hand-book of almost any of them and you will find a paragraph something like the following, which I copy from the report of 1862 of the Mutual Life Insurance Company of New York, then as now the foremost of American companies:

" Surrender of Life Policies.

"Should the original motive for effecting an assurance in this company cease before the termination of life, the party may surrender his policy, after it has run two years, for an equitable consideration, which may be paid to him by the company on its surrender."

Though in this wording "*may*" is not the most efficient

auxiliary verb that could have been selected, as a matter of
fact a vast amount of surrender value has been paid by this
company, and is paid, and so equitably withal, that speculators have very little chance of making money by buying
and keeping up its policies, even if American law would
allow such transactions. That the cessation of the original
motive for insurance in any individual case is a very important and not very improbable contingency, is obvious enough
from the fact that at the very time when the report above
quoted from was made there were outstanding only 12,258
policies out of 24,929 which had been issued by that company. Considering that most of these 12,671 policies which
had ceased to exist were whole-life policies, paying for the
time-being largely beyond the risk incurred on them by the
company, the question of the " equitable consideration " to be
received from the company on the cancelment was a very interesting one, involving in the aggregate a very large sum of
money. It grows more and more interesting, since the cessation of motive to insure and any divergence from equity in
the rule for settling surrender value must both increase with
the age of the company. It is interesting to every outsider
who, by any possibility, may hereafter be tempted to insure.
It cannot but be interesting, even when one is about entering
an earthly paradise, to know by what gate and on what terms
he can get out, in case he should find it necessary or desirable to do so.

The gentlemen who have the executive management of
life-insurance companies may not see fit to notice this conundrum immediately. It is very proper that they should
take abundant time to consider it, perhaps to consult with
each other about it, and avail themselves of all the light
which science or the nature of things can furnish to aid
them. If after they have done so they cannot give an answer consistent with the present practice in any company,
then assuredly a revolution in their business is at hand,

and the sooner they welcome it the better for themselves, as well as their constituents.

Conundrum.

By the law of New York the reserve on an ordinary life policy for $1,000, entered at 35, at the end of its second year, is $20.01. (It has paid two premiums, say of $26.87 each, though the law does not regard the premiums actually paid in fixing the reserve.) Suppose the "equitable consideration" which may be paid to the insured on surrender is only *one cent*, the twenty dollars being justly and necessarily retained by the company to compensate it for the loss of a good life. Now, in the case of the surrender of another policy for $1,000, also entered at 35, and which, having paid forty premiums, has a legal reserve of $653.17, let us know why any *more* than twenty dollars should be deducted from said reserve. In other words, if *one cent* is the just surrender value of the former policy, can anything less than $633.17 be the "equitable consideration" for the surrender of the latter, and if so, why?

After the defeat of the Surrender Value Bill in the Massachusetts Senate, it became very obvious that no legislature could be expected ever to enact a law which should make the life-insurance autocracies more directly responsible to their theoretical constituents, or which should forbid the issue of policies that are the most profitable. to agents and officers who share commissions with them. These autocracies have grown too rich to be stinted of their most fattening pabulum. They have too much money to lend, or place "where it will do good," as the phrase now is. The existing policy-holders, have no interest in the matter, for no legislature can modify existing contracts. The future policy-holders, born and unborn, are an unconscious crowd, incapable of lobbying, and who do not even pretend to have any rights which legislatures are bound to provide for.

The only hope that the friends of fair play and honest business can have is in so enlightening the public mind that life-insurance agents, however tempted by exorbitant commissions, shall find themselves unable to entice *any body* into a bargain not fit to be made.

It was to this problem that the writer addressed himself immediately after the defeat of the Surrender Value Bill. He had done what he could to correct the blunder committed by him, as much as any one, in the Act of 1861. The result of his labors and consultations with the ablest experts in this country, was published in a series of 268 working or practical tables, in which all the values, important to be known, are pre-calculated for every year of the policy, preceded by a popular explanation. As the tabular work is necessarily cumbrous and expensive, the whole of the explanation will be given in the succeeding pages with two or three specimen tables.

The critical reader will undoubtedly be disgusted, before the close of this volume, with its vast amount of repetition, but it is intended for those who need line upon line, and it must be remembered that the nonsense it seeks to explode has been repeated in many shapes many millions of times.

Chapter IV.

Savings Bank Life Insurance.

The necessity of maintaining a premium reserve, according to some fixed rule, is now generally acknowledged by American life insurance companies.

It is not so generally acknowledged that this necessarily implies that, whether the policy-holder is allowed to regard himself to any extent as a depositor or not, the company must treat every premium on a policy extending for more than one year as if a certain part of it, more or less, were a mere savings bank or trust-fund deposit, with only this difference from an ordinary one, that it cannot be withdrawn till the death of the insured or the stipulated termination of the policy. It is then withdrawn only as a part, or the whole, of the claim. Hence, to the extent of that part of the claim which the company will pay out of the reserve in its hands, in any year when the death may occur, the party may be said to insure himself in that year. Hence, too, if the policy is made payable at the end of a certain year, whether the party dies in it or lives through it, he insures himself during that last year to the full amount of the claim.* In other words so far as his net premium is concerned, he contributes nothing in that year to pay the claims on other policies, nor do the other policies contribute anything to pay his. This is the logical sequence of a fixed rule of reserve, and no cavil at

---

* The net premium is always calculated on the supposition that the death-claim will be paid at the *end* of the policy year in which the death occurs. Whatever the company loses by paying it earlier, has to come out of margin, or surplus from vitality or interest.

the terms "savings bank" or "self-insurance" will avail to set it aside.

It is quite true that, so long as a policy-holder does not participate at all in surplus and has no right to a surrender value before the expiration of his policy, the distinction between the insurance and self-insurance on his policy is of no practical interest to him. All he wants to know in that case is, that the claim will be paid when it occurs. But the company, to be able honestly to assure him of this, must know that it has in reserve a certain portion of his past premiums, and how much it will have to reserve of future ones. *It* must also know in advance the relation of the insurance to the self-insurance on its various policies, in order to know what it can afford to give to procure them.

But whenever policy-holders are allowed in any way to participate in surplus, and still more when they are allowed any surrender value in case of discontinuance, then the inevitable savings-bank aspect of the company, as distinct from its insurance aspect, begins seriously to interest them. Many of them cannot afford to have the distinction ignored, because the equitable dealing which has been promised them in general terms, depends upon it. It has in fact become important for each one of them to know just how far the company, under his policy, acts towards him as an insurance company, and how far as a savings bank,—how far *it* insures him from year to year, and how far *he*, by his payments beyond the current cost of the company's risks, from year to year, insures himself. Under any policy certainly payable at the end of a shorter or longer term, or at previous death, if the premium paid at the beginning of each year is not restricted to the company's risk of having to pay the claim in that year,—which it never is,—it, in point of fact, assumes only a decreasing series of risks, ending in none at all the last year; and the insured, by the excess of his payments over the costs of the company's risks, at interest in the hands

of the company, provides for an increasing series of comple-
ments, ending with the full amount of the sum insured. Now
if the insured is to receive any surplus, anything at all besides the indemnity stipulated, whether that surplus is to be
paid in cash, in additional insurance or by shortening the
term of the policy, the equitable share of it will depend upon
the relation of the insurance to the self-insurance of the policy, and the distinct effect on each of the experience of the
company. On the insurance, surplus arises only from the
death-claims and expenses of the insurance being less than
were provided for, or less than the expenses and normal cost
of carrying the risks. On the self-insurance, it arises only
from profits on the investments beyond what was assumed in
the rule of reserve after deducting the cost of managing the
fund. There may be surplus on the self-insurance when
there is none on the insurance and *vice versa*. If the surplus
arises wholly out of insurance and no extra interest has been
realized on the self-insurance fund, it would be a very queer
equity which would give a dividend of any kind to a policy
having no insurance at all upon it. And so of the opposite
case, in which all the surplus should arise from extra interest
and none from insurance, to give equal dividends to equal
premiums, or equal policies, then would be just as equitable
as to give equal dividends to all the depositors of a savings
bank, without regard to the amount of their deposits. By a
distinction between insurance and self-insurance a demonstrable equity in the assignment of surplus may be secured, or a
fair approximation to it, and in no other conceivable way.

This, in case the premiums are so high as probably to yield
surplus—and only with such premiums can mutual life insurance be conducted with desirable certainty—it is very important for the policy-holder to know. Perhaps there is no
other way of enabling him to understand the contract he
makes, and to be satisfied with equitable treatment as to surplus and surrender when he gets it, than to analyze fully the

business on his policy into its distinct elements of insurance and self-insurance, and let him see how the two, on the assumptions of the premium and reserve, stand related for each future year of its possible continuance. Apart from fixing a surrender value, this binds the company no tighter than it is already bound by fidelity to its assumptions as to mortality and interest, if not by statute law as to reserve. Can the company bind itself to a fixed rule of surrender value, so as to make what has been called self-insurance substantially a savings-bank deposit?

The policy-holder who takes a policy binding the company to insure him, sick or well, for a long number of years, must be well aware that its ability to do so will depend upon its continuing to have a very large number of members, and that every healthy member who leaves it, diminishes its strength and stability, more or less, according to what he might be expected to pay towards death-claims, if he did not leave. Hence it is very absurd to say that a company can afford to release a healthy member from his contract whenever he pleases to retire, and allow him to withdraw his self-insurance fund, without making *any* compensation to the company for its loss in the non-fulfilment of his contract. This loss has no relation whatever to the self-insurance or reserve, for that could be of no use to the other members if he remained, being wholly devoted to meet the party's own claim; but it has direct relation to the risks contracted to be borne by the company and the successive payments to be made on account of them. The present value of those payments, or normal costs of insurance, discounted on the same assumptions of mortality and interest as are used in computing the reserve, or what may be called the insurance value of the policy as distinct from the self-insurance value or reserve, must be the basis of estimating the company's loss by a withdrawal. The self-insurance value is only a security in the hands of the company, more or less ample, for the payment of this damage.

When this damage or surrender charge is paid, the security is released; and the whole savings-bank deposit is withdrawn.

Let it be understood that the insurance value is not the charge, but the basis of the charge. For when the insurance value is lost, there is a cancelment of the company's liability gained, and if the retiring life were no better than the average, the gain would fully offset the loss. We have only to provide a charge on the assumption that it is better. If it is better, the gain will not fully offset the loss, and the difference will be proportioned to the insurance value. Hence the surrender charge must be some percentage of the insurance value, either variable or invariable.

This is by no means an innovation in principle, but only a new mode of applying, or rather looking at, a principle long ago accepted. Though the usual policy—a form borrowed from England—expressly excludes the right of the policy-holder to withdraw *any* part of the premiums previously paid, in case of his forfeiting the right to further insurance by non-payment of premium or otherwise, in practice, in this country, the reserve has always been returned, either in cash when applied for while the policy was in force, or in premium notes, the company having deducted more or less of the cash part of it—if there was any—as a compensation for its loss. The only variation of the practice from the savings-bank theory has been that the companies have not estimated their loss with any regard to the insurance value withdrawn, but have erroneously regarded it as having some relation or other to the reserve or self-insurance value. The grotesque absurdity of this, only waited for the short-term endowment insurance business, which has so enormously increased of late, to bring it fully to light.

That the principle of recognizing the right of the policy-holder in the reserve, as a savings-bank deposit, which it is the object of the present work to apply more correctly in

5

practice, has been held by authority worthy of the highest respect, may be sufficiently proved by a quotation from a pamphlet issued by the New England Mutual Life Insurance Company in 1845, from the pen of its first President, Hon. Willard Phillips, LL. D., the author of the well-known treatise on Insurance Law. He opens by saying, " The object of this institution, in respect to insurance for the whole life, is similar to that of savings banks," and before he closes he has the following passage, which clearly recognizes that, to a certain not distinctly defined extent, its method. also embraces a savings-bank feature :—

" It sometimes happens, that the motive for making insurance ceases before the policy has expired. Instances will also occasionally occur, of persons being disappointed of the means of paying the premium, and so being liable to forfeit their policies. In any such case, the company will consent to a surrender of the policy upon fair terms, if an application is made for that purpose before the policy is forfeited. Where the policy is made for a longer period than it has actually run, the amount of premium paid upon it will have been greater than if it had been made only for such time.

" Suppose, for example, that a person of the age of twenty-five years has insured himself for his whole life in the sum of one thousand dollars, and at the end of seven years, wishes, for whatever reason, to surrender his policy. If he had taken the policy originally for that period, he would have paid, in the whole, in annual premiums and deposits, $77.70, but taking the policy for his whole life, he has paid in and deposited $138.60, making a difference of $60.90. In this case the company has paid out the $77.70 ; for, though the person insured survives the period of seven years, yet if one hundred have been insured for that time, one of them has died and the premium must be such as to enable the company to pay the loss. This is the principle upon which the premium for a policy for that period is calculated. The party proposing to surrender has had the good fortune to live, and the surviving family of the one who has died has had the good fortune to be provided for. But the company cannot afford to square the account by merely striking this balance, and paying back the whole $60.90 to a person who, being in good health,

wishes to surrender his policy, since another, who was insured
for his whole life, and whose health has been impaired during
the seven years, might choose not to surrender his policy;
and the company should avail itself of the policy on which
the risk has turned out favorably, to make up for that on
which the risk has proved unfavorable. Some reservation
must, therefore, on this account, be made by the company out
of the amount, whatever it may be, which, in the above example, is represented by $60.90; since, otherwise, the com-
pany would be prejudiced by agreeing to the surrender. As
to the amount of this reservation, it is evident that no precise
rule can be laid down, but it is obvious that, after a policy for
the whole life has begun to acquire a present value, that value
goes on increasing and regularly approximating every year
towards the amount insured, and making such approximation
more and more rapidly, as the party insured advances in age,
and his bodily infirmities increase, and the increase of mortality becomes developed; so that, if it becomes necessary
for him to avail himself of such value, that necessity is most
likely to come upon him at a period of life when it has made
a near approximation to the amount insured, and when, if he
had not reserved to himself this resource, he most probably
would have had no resource whatever. The above sugges-
tions are made for the purpose of giving to the holder of a
policy for life, the means of making a proximate estimate of
its value from time to time." *

The fact that the method of the company embraces the two
functions of insurance and savings bank is here sufficiently
admitted. The only defects are the assumed impossibility of
distinguishing between them by any "precise rule" as to the
amount of "reservation" or surrender ·charge, and making
the right to receive surrender value—or withdraw deposits—
depend on applying for it while the insurance is in force.
Plainly, if there can be any title apart from the terms of the
policy to receive such value, it will be as good the moment
after, or any reasonable time after, the forfeiture of the right

---

* See, also, the Fifth Annual Report (1848) of the Directors, where
the interest of members in the "reserved funds " is expressly admitted.

to be further insured, as it was before, and cannot depend for its existence on the company's being notified to pay it.

Let us inquire whether there is any good reason why there cannot be a "precise rule" as to the *maximum* surrender charge. If there is, it must hold equally good against fixing any precise premiums or terms of entrance. It is no more reasonable to attempt to grade and value individually the good lives that seek to withdraw, and have a sliding scale of surrender charges without a *maximum* limit, than to do the same thing in regard to those who seek to enter, and have a sliding scale of premiums without a *minimum* limit. If we have admitted all unexceptionable lives at the same premium for the age, it must be admitted that the best of them will probably pay more dearly for the same benefit than the worst. This, if it is an evil, or a departure from equity, is necessary in a system which is founded on human ignorance of future events, and could not honestly exist if this ignorance had not considerable density. But if, on this system we have made the healthiest of these insured persons pay for several years the same as the least healthy, that is, more than the cost of his insurance, and then, when he applies for surrender, we grow suddenly wise, and charge him more than we would an average good life, we cannot logically refuse to credit him, against this excess, with the excess of his past payments. Here the case becomes as broad as it is long.

In all good faith and charity, is the claim that the company must grade the surrender charge according to its notions of the degree of vitality in the retiring life, any better than the pretence that applicants for insurance, in a normal state of health and with no apparent predisposition to disease, can be graded by a study of their ancestors,—multiplying back into the past, as an innumerable dim cloud of dusty witnesses, from which, according to theory, ought to converge upon the living individual all possible diseases, including longevity? This argument proves decidedly too much in both cases.

As to compensating the company on the whole, and sufficiently, for the loss of good lives, it is quite plain that it can be done as well by a precise charge as a variable one, if we only make the precise charge high enough. Because, it is impossible for the company to lose more (this, of course, applies to a mutual company, in which surplus is supposed to be divided as fast as it arises), than the whole of the insurance value. And even a charge of one hundred per cent. of the insurance value, would be a great improvement, in point of equity, upon the present ill-founded and indefinite rule.

But, fix the charge as we will, and admit that it is sufficient to compensate the company for its loss, it is pertinaciously contended that guaranteeing *any* surrender value at all is offering a premium for lapse, and that it is wiser to offer nothing, but when a case arises treat it "on its own merits." Very well. How do we get at the merits? How do we know that a life that was admitted as good is now better? And if we do know it, would we, on the strength of this knowledge, reduce the premium? If not, and certainly we should not, how can we say to the man, Though your vitality is not good enough to justify us in reducing your premium if you stay in, it is so good and so much better than the average that you must pay an extra charge for going out?

The plain truth is, that the officers of the company have not knowledge enough to make a distinction between the vitalities of what may be called unexceptionable lives. Neither, on the other hand, have the best lives any such knowledge of their own vitality as to get the advantage of the company in selecting themselves out. From the necessities of human ignorance and other circumstances, the game is a pretty fair one on both sides. The fact is, that men stick to their policies as long as they have the *motive* and the *means* to continue, and when those fail, or either of them, they will discontinue without much regard to their state of health, whether the surrender value returned is equitable or not. But if it is not equitable, the credit and popularity of the company is likely to suffer as much, in the long run, as the purse of the retiring policy-holder.

If there is any force in these considerations, the fairest measure of the loss of the company by the non-fulfilment of a policy-contract, is, what it will cost to procure another of equal insurance value, on a life equally good. If the charge is made unquestionably more than this, the stability of the company cannot possibly be impaired by guaranteeing a surrender value, unless we suppose the public demand for insurance is to cease, which is the same thing as supposing that civilized society is to come to an end, or some miraculous change is to happen to it.

What does it cost to get insurance value? What is, or what ought to be its market price? Much of it has, in point of fact, cost too much. Most of it, however, has actually been obtained for three or four per cent. of itself. The scheme here proposed assumes that the company will be fully indemnified, on the average, for its loss of insurance value on the best lives by a charge of eight per cent. on the same.

Let us see how this rule would apply to the case put by Judge Phillips. The four per cent. reserve on a policy for $1,000 entered at twenty-five, at the end of the seventh year is $58.53. Its insurance value at that time is $192.41, of which eight per cent. is $15.39. A new policy entered at twenty-five for $1,432, payable at sixty-five or previous death, will have the same insurance value, $192.41, and the annual premium of this in the New England Life Insurance Company, would be $31.51. $15.39 is nearly fifty per cent. of this, or about twice as much as the company has to pay for procuring a policy as valuable to it as the one it lost. The new policy is indeed a little more valuable to it, from being limited to sixty-five. The policy which it lost extending over the whole life, a part of its insurance value consists of insurance to be done beyond the insurable interest, and is of a somewhat inferior quality. It is on this account that a company can undoubtedly afford to give a little more, in proportion to its insurance value, for an endowment insurance of moderate term, than for a whole-life insurance,—though by no means several times as much, as is commonly done.

Let us suppose an army—an army of occupation for example—in which sound health is the main desideratum, and which is recruitable at so much a head. Is it weakened, by the "precise rule," that a discharge can be had by paying twice the cost of procuring a substitute satisfactory to the surgeon? Would the sanitary condition of the army be lowered by such a rule? It is easy to see how the army might be weakened, by mustering out soldiers for money, if no recruits could be obtained, and so a life-insurance company might be weakened, as such, by members retiring, if none came in. If all public demand for life insurance should cease, the more the old members should retire, the sooner would the business come to an end, but not a disastrous one.

To recur again to the army: it is plain enough that enlistment is unpopular in proportion to the difficulty of getting out, should one change his mind after some experience of camp-life. Any reasonable alleviation of that difficulty will reduce the cost of getting recruits. So in life insurance: nothing has more enhanced the difficulty of adding new members, than the exorbitant sacrifices that often have to be made by old members who have paid their full premiums in cash, when they have occasion to retire.

If a man is able to take a policy, and will really be benefited by it, a stipulated surrender value, which is reasonable and business-like, will remove from his mind every obstructive doubt, and there will be no need of expending upon him costly visions of dividends, which it would be death to the company to realize. To persuade any prudent man to take a policy on the present terms, with no rule of surrender that can be understood or stated in advance in figures, it is necessary to work him up to such a pitch of enthusiasm or infatuation that he shall entirely overlook the fact that his circumstances may change, and he may cease to need insurance before the term of his proposed policy expires. This is a tedious and costly process. In the aggregate, it now costs in the United States many millions of dollars a year.

In fire insurance a great part of the business flows into the companies spontaneously. The savings banks proper pay nothing to obtain theirs, and it is immense and quite permanent. Life insurance companies, to which a great multiplication of risks is specially important, will undoubtedly always have to pay something for obtaining business, or at least till State legislatures reduce the rate at which they create new companies. But by adopting the savings-bank plan, the expense of getting it can unquestionably be greatly reduced, so that even the soliciting agent will not be the loser by the low commissions.

It is believed that the following tables furnish as copious a choice of policies as is desirable, and a restriction of the business of a company to these will greatly simplify its accounts and calculations. From fifteen to thirty years of age persons will have the option of eight different policies; from thirty to thirty-five, of seven; from thirty-five to forty, of six, &c., with different proportions of insurance and self-insurance. The lowest premium will turn out the best in case of an early demise, although it pays most to expenses while it continues. But the highest premium will prove best, if the party lives through the term, on the principle that the more he insures himself the less he has to pay towards the expenses of the company. And it will always be better, if one can, to take a shorter policy at a higher premium, than a longer one at a lower premium, if one is to live and surrender at the end of a given number of years, because in the latter case, one must have paid expenses in proportion to the larger amount of insurance contracted for. For example : a person at twenty-five, has the option of taking eight different policies, of which, the terms vary from fifteen to fifty years, and the premiums from $22.45 to $56.07 per $1,000.

If he takes that of the longest term, paying $22.45 per annum, and at the end of ten years surrenders, he will get back $83.58 in cash, the rest of the $224.50 and interest, supposing there have been no dividends, having gone for the death-claims of others, the working expenses and the surrender charge. And suppose that he had annually deposited in a savings bank, yielding five per cent. interest, the difference ($33.62) between the lowest and highest premium, he might then have in addition to the $83.58, the amount of $444.02, making $527.60, as the residual of his expenditure of $560.70. If he takes the shortest policy, which will cost him just that, the residual at the end of ten years will be $585.31, a gain in this event, over the other arrangement, of $57.71. It is very true that there would be about thirty-seven per cent. more of insurance done by the company in the ten years under the long policy, which would have made it a better arrangement to die on. The point is, that the short one is the better to live through on, or to surrender on, and in fact better than the long one with the savings bank added, which can by no means be said of the present short-term endowment policies, with the usual rates of premium and conditions of surrender.

Under the present system, unless a person is quite sure that he will be able to continue his policy, so as to share the profits of the forfeiture of other policies,* and will need to

* Betting on persistence when the persistent members are sure to win, is undoubtedly profitable, whatever may be said of its morality. It is by no means a necessary or graceful feature of life insurance, and

continue it, it is always best for him to take the whole-life or longest endowment policy, because he can always invest the difference between the premium of that and a shorter term more profitably than in the life-insurance company,—in a savings bank for example. But, on the contrary, under the system of savings-bank life insurance here proposed, no person who needs insurance, and has anything to pay for it, can afford to make any deposit whatever in a savings bank.

As life insurance is now conducted, beyond any question, one-fourth of the premium paid into the life insurance companies had better be paid into savings banks, as it could be without at all reducing the insurance effected. To illustrate: in 1870 life insurance to the amount of about two thousand

---

it is more congenial to the avowed object of the institution to avoid all needless departure from the legal maxim, *suum cuique*. But as this betting is now managed, the persistent members, as a body, do not win in all cases of forfeiture, and supposing they do win on the whole, an individual among them is by no means sure of receiving his fair share of the winnings, if any one knows what that is.

For example: when a company holds premium notes on a policy beyond its equitable cash surrender value, it will lose by forfeiture, unless it collects the notes, a process that is never thought of, much less effected. Again, when it gives a paid-up policy, presumed to be a fair reversion of the net value or reserve, it never gains much, and sometimes loses a little, because it takes no account of its loss of insurance value in the operation.

Supposing that I is the insurance value per dollar of the existing policy at the date of the change, and z is the proper percentage of it for a surrender charge, and I' is the insurance value per dollar of a paid-up policy at the party's present age; then for an existing policy of S dollars, which has run t years, the company can afford to give, on a good life,

only $S\dfrac{H_{x+t}-zI}{II_{x+t}-zI'}$, and would give too much if it gave $S\dfrac{H_{x+t}}{II_{x+t}}$. When on a policy having m possible payments it gives a paid-up policy for $\dfrac{t}{m}$ S, it often gives more than the former value, even when it gives less than the latter.

millions was in force in the United States, and the premium paid was about ninety millions. Sixty-eight millions would have procured just as much insurance, on policies of longer terms or slower payment, and the difference of twenty-two millions, in the absence of savings-bank life insurance, would much more profitably have been deposited in ordinary savings banks. On the other hand, as life insurance ought to be conducted, probably one-quarter or one-half the deposits in the savings banks could be transferred to the life-insurance companies, with great benefit to the families of the depositors.

How to Adjust the Premiums.

The light of antiquity tells us that we shall go safest in the middle of things. There is no going in the middle, in life insurance, without providing in the premiums for death-claims occurring somewhat faster than we expect them, and for interest being less and expenses more than they need be. Putting the working expenses out of the account, we shall have a middle path in providing for death-claims, if we assume, in calculating the net premiums, only four per cent. interest and the actuaries' mortality, which has proved considerably higher than the average experience of American companies. This is the well-established basis for computing net premiums, and there seems to be no occasion to unsettle it in providing for savings-bank life insurance.

But the margin to be added to the net premium, as a provision for expenses and extraordinary contingencies, should obviously be modified to adapt it to the principles above stated.

The expenditures of a life-insurance company may be classified under the following heads :—

1. The death-claims.
2. Surrender values, including endowments.
3. Cost of managing the reserve or self-insurance fund.

4. Cost of collecting the premiums.

5. All other working expenses, including the cost of procuring business.

The first three heads are amply provided for by the net premiums and their interest. The last two only are to be provided for by added margin. The cost of collecting the premiums may as fairly be proportioned to their amount in this business as any other, whether they are devoted to insurance or self-insurance.

All the other working expenses should be assessed in proportion to the insurance value of the policy for the year in which they occur, because that value represents the comparative interest which each member has in the company, as an insurance company, in that year. To provide for this and nothing more, would be to add a margin varying with the insurance value from year to year, which would have the great inconvenience of making the gross premiums variable. To avoid this, as well as to avoid extending the insurance beyond the insurable interest, no policy is extended beyond the age of SEVENTY-FIVE. Policies limited to that age do not increase in insurance value much, if any, so that a constant margin added, proportionate to the *initial* insurance value, will gradually become more and more ample for its purpose as the policy increases in age, and of course will be more and more returned in dividend, if not needed for adverse contingencies. This redundancy of margin in the advanced years of a policy is far from being undesirable as an additional resource against adversity in a remote future. In the following tables, four per cent. of the initial insurance value is first added to the net premium as a provision for expenses under the fifth head, and then one thirty-ninth of itself is added to the sum, to make the gross premium, on the supposition that two and one-half per cent. of it will be allowed as the cost of collection.* If it should be objected that so

* Adopting the notation used in the preface to the revised edition of

slender a margin does not give motive-power enough to work
the machine, and the percentages added should be increased,
let it be considered that they make the premiums of the longest terms higher than they are now, and no one pretends
that a company wholly consisting of such policies could not
stand, or that the premiums have not sufficient motive-power.
The premiums of the shorter terms are lower, but they have
more margin in proportion to the insurance to be done on
them than on those of the longer terms, for the collection-fee
is added to the whole. If they are too low, it is because a
savings bank cannot be run for two and one-half per cent. on
each deposit at the time of its reception, and one per cent.
per annum of the whole amount on deposit.

The expenses of the fourth and fifth heads must, of course,
be confined within that margin at first, and must bear a decreasing ratio to it as the policies grow older. It is obvious
enough that, on this plan, if the expenses should be excessive, assessing them in proportion to insurance value, would
show *negative* contributions to surplus from policies of large
insurance value, and small self-insurance, while, at the same
time, there might be a preponderance of positive contributions from policies of small insurance value and large self-
insurance. This would require a new assessment of these
negatives or deficiencies, on the policies of positive contribution, and this would produce another smaller crop of negatives, to be at last reduced to zero by repeating the process,
before the divisible surplus could be equitably distributed. In
fact, it might at last amount substantially to assessing the

my Valuation Tables, the general form of the gross premium, P_x, for a
Savings-Bank Insurance Policy will be

$$P_x = {}_{x+n}\pi_x + z \times {}_{x+n}I_x + \frac{y\,({}_{x+n}\pi_x + z \times {}_{x+n}I_x)}{1-y}$$

the first term of the second member being the net premium; the second,
the provision for that part of the expenses which is to be assessed in
proportion to insurance value; and the third, the provision for a collection-fee to be allowed as a constant percentage y of the gross premium.

insurance expenses, according to the margins, a manifest hardship to the holders of the short-term policies approaching their termination, whose margin, small as it is, after deducting the uniform collection fee of two and one-half per cent., is still very large in proportion to the insurance that remains to be done on them. The proper course is to restrict the expenses to such a degree that *negative* contributions shall not appear. The actuary will have no difficulty, with the analysis of the following tables applied to each policy at the beginning of any year, to inform the company within what limit the aggregate expenses of the year must fall, to avoid negative contributions.* It has been found, in almost all financial institutions, a wise thing to restrict expenses by definite pre-appropriation. There is more need of this in life insurance, because the death-claims, which cannot be restricted, must be expected to fluctuate considerably, both in number and amount, and there is always a possibility that they may slightly exceed the normal cost of insurance so as to require some part of the margin.

The Advantages of the System.

1. The policies will be more persistent, because every one will know at the start what he is to expect, and will know that the longer he stays in the less it will cost him to get out; whereas, under the old system, he soon learns that the longer he stays in the more it will cost him to get out.

2. When any one leaves the company he will go out satisfied, having been dealt with on prescribed and pre-understood

---

* Thus, supposing that S stands for the savings-bank deposits on outstanding policies, P the aggregate gross premiums on the same, payable during the year, and I their aggregate insurance value, the expenses, exclusive of commissions on new policies, must be limited to $\frac{S}{100} + .025 \times P + .04 \times I$, to avoid negative contributions on some of the policies, in case the death-claims of the year should equal the normal ones.

terms. The company will thus avoid the back-water from retiring members, which is now troublesome, if not overwhelming.

3. Equitable dividends, should there be any surplus to divide, can be made intelligible to any member. He is supposed to have a table, like one in this work, analyzing all his annual payments. The company, by means of similar tables, so keeps its books that it can tell, by a mere footing of them, what is its required reserve, what the insurance value of all its policies, and what the normal cost of carrying all its risks. It can tell, at the end of its fiscal year, what has been its average rate of interest, what its death-claims are in excess of the self-insurance on them, and what its working.expenses, over one per cent. of the self-insurance fund and two and one-half per cent. of the premium receipts, have been. Let us suppose the actual interest has been six per cent., the actual cost of insurance four-fifths of the normal cost, and the expenses, less the cost of collection, three per cent. of the insurance value. If this experience of the company's fiscal year is to be applied to all policies whose policy-years ended in it, to determine the contribution to surplus which is to be returned as dividend at the settlement of the next, or the succeeding premium (which is near enough to equity, as a practical rule*), each policy-holder may easily calculate his own dividend, or at any rate easily satisfy himself whether what the company assigns him is correct, knowing the several factors above stated.

For example : suppose his policy is for $1,000, payable at death or fifty, entered at twenty-five and has closed its ninth year, within this fiscal year of the company. Referring to

* Under this rule, a retiring policy-holder necessarily forfeits any surplus that may have arisen on his policy during its last year. With this the surrender charge and the rule that surrender value shall be paid only at the end of a policy-year, the life-insurance savings bank will be safer against panic, or a run upon it, than any other.

the table (No. 4), we find his reserve at the end of his eighth year $207.49, to which was added at the beginning of the ninth, $22.15, making the self-insurance fund at the beginning of the ninth year $229.64. Four per cent. of the interest was required to make this $238.83 at the end of the year, and one per cent. to pay for managing the fund, so there is $2.30 of surplus from the self-insurance. The normal cost of insuring him that year was $6.53, of which one-fifth or $1.31 was saved, which is so much more of surplus from vitality. The insurance value at the beginning of the year was $54.30. Three per cent. of this would be $1.63 for expenses, to which if two and one-half per cent. of the premium be added for collection, we have $2.45 to be deducted from the margin, $4.23, which leaves a surplus from that source of $1.78. Thus the surplus which belongs to him is,—

From self-insurance, ...	. $2 30
From insurance, ...	. 1 31
From margin, ...	. 1 78
	—— $5 39

In the same way, if the policy had ended its first year within the fiscal year, its surplus would have been,—

From self-insurance, ...	. $0 21
From insurance, ...	. 1 46
From margin, ...	. 86
	—— $2 53

And for its twentieth year it would have been,—

From self-insurance, ...	. $6 70
From insurance, ...	. 68
From margin, ...	. 3 09
	——$10 47

Executive officers who have the task of explaining "contribution" dividends to thousands of members, will not be a great many years in finding out the advantage of this arrangement.

Other advantages of great public import might be named,

such as diminishing to the degree of ordinary saving banks the necessity, difficulty and expense of governmental super-vision, and removing the mystery which now deprives the business of the popularity it deserves; but enough, it is believed, has been said to satisfy all conscientious life-insurance men, who understand human nature and seek its welfare, that it is worthy of a fair trial.

THE VALUE OF LIFE INSURANCE.

It must not be inferred from what precedes, that life insurance, as it exists in this country, is not worthy of the immense confidence it has received. The civilization of this continent has no institution of which it has a better right to be proud. It is the standing together, shoulder to shoulder, of hosts of manly men, to defend each others' homes from that enemy who shoots on the sly and in the dark. It is the realization of fraternity without the destruction of independence and individuality. It is a charity without cant, which enriches the giver and does not humiliate the receiver. Thanks to the care which has been taken to maintain reserve at a high standard, looking at the business as a whole, there is no hollowness. What it has been doing, it can continue to do. The world has been delighted with itself at the degree and promptitude of the alleviation which has met the Chicago calamity. American life insurance silently, every year, meets suffering of almost equal amount and deeper intensity, with nearly all the alleviation money can give. The organization, in advance, of this relief, and the certainty of its application in case of need, give it a current value to all parties concerned, which far transcends the ninety or one hundred millions a year which it costs. Here are nearly a million of men whose aggregate material wealth, all told, does not perhaps exceed five hundred millions, who by this institution have possession of two thousand millions in addition, immediately available for the only purpose for which they really need or could enjoy it. This is better than a rich uncle to a young man who has not a rich father; and if he has both, and also the noble ambition to paddle his own canoe, it is better than a share in a gold mine.

The institution may have defects to be supplied, or excrescences to be pruned away, but any charlatanry which would depreciate its value, or undermine public faith in it, would be equally deplorable and unpardonable. The aim and reasoning of the foregoing pages will be entirely misapprehended if they are supposed to favor the conclusion that the holders of existing policies had better relinquish them. The number of those who could wisely take such a course has never been one-half or one-quarter as great as of those who have taken it, nor is it likely that good reasons for withdrawal will increase.

Life insurance is so good, is capable of a so much wider application, and is so thoroughly in unison with the spirit of our republican society, that it cannot fail, by and by, to be understood by everybody and enjoyed by everybody who needs it, as universally as the various arrangements by which steam and lightning are utilized. What is wanted is, that the school-house and the press—the universal educators—shall take up the matter, not in the interest of the companies or their agents, but in that of the public and its coming generations. The companies have nothing to fear, but everything to hope from the most thorough discussion of their plans and the exposure of all the details of their management. In borrowing the science of their business from England, they wisely did not borrow that instinct of corporation-secrecy which prevails in it there with very unfortunate results. They have expended liberally to enlighten the public, and have welcomed governmental investigation to an extent that is almost ludicrously superfluous, and threatens to be more so. It is not at all creditable to the press that it should so little aid them in this matter,—rarely speaking at all of its

own motion, and then too often in a style to make it profitable
to the public as well as the companies to buy its silence.

Notwithstanding all this, the business has had a development in this country which a mere reader of newspapers finds
it difficult to believe. And this development has been, in the
main, sound and healthy, because the companies have been
so much more ready to meet intelligent criticism than the
press to apply it. The error into which they have inadvert-
ently drifted, of allowing too much motive-power on the more
self-insuring policies, and the other borrowed error of putting
the surrender charge on the wrong basis,—making it in regard to what *has been* paid, instead of what *is to be* paid,—
will certainly be corrected in due time. They only wait the
waking up of a little disinterested discussion. When that is
aroused, there will also disappear that other original excres-
cence of insuring lives beyond threescore and fifteen. There
will be no use of issuing savings-bank policies beyond that
limit, because they would be sure to surrender then, if not
sooner,—unless the disease of which Methuselah died is to
become epidemic.

Explanation of Tables.—Most persons perceive the relation
to each other of lines more readily than of numbers. Hence
a complicated problem which fails to be understood when
stated by numerals, or other symbols, may often be made intelligible to everybody by diagrams or chalking on a black-
board.

Mathematical experts in life insurance will smile at the
clumsiness of the following illustrations, but they should re-
member there was a time before they became familiar with
algebra, when this ladder would have been the easiest way to
the spot where they now stand. It is not, however, designed
for them, but for persons having only the commonest knowledge of arithmetic, and eyes to recognize the proportion of
things.

A man commonly insures a certain sum on his life, just as he does on his house, by paying the same premium year after year. Yet the risk of a loss on the life is very different at different ages, while that of one on the house commonly remains the same. It is this páying for a variable risk with a constant premium, which is the peculiarity of life insurance and the source of all its mystery. The natural way would be to make the premium vary from year to year according to the variation of the risk, but this variation is so peculiar, as we shall presently see, that this natural way is hardly practi-cable.

By the Actuaries' Rate of Mortality, which does not differ materially from any other used for the purpose of insuring life, the average probability of dying at any age is given from 10 to 100, beyond which there is assumed to be no chance of living worth taking into account.* If the question be, how to insure for life $1,000 on a healthy person aged 32, let us first try the natural method. He has, according to our assumed scale of mortality, 68 possible years to live. Let us (see Plate I.) divide the line A B into 68 equal parts to represent his future years of life. Let the perpendicular line A C and the 68 perpendiculars parallel to it be divided into 100 equal parts by lines drawn parallel to the base, and let each of these perpendicular parts represent 10 units, so that the whole height of the parallelogram may represent either one thousand persons or one thousand dollars, as we please. If the perpendiculars represent one thousand persons living to commence the ages from 32 to 100, the series of heavy black lines standing on A B, being very short, increasing very gradually at first, and faster and faster by and by, will nearly represent the number of persons expected to die out of 1,000 at each age. In other words, the ratio of the thick, dark part of the perpendicular to the whole of it, at each age, is the risk

---

* See Appendix for Actuaries' Rate of Mortality, and the natural premiums, at four per cent.

of dying ˚at that age, though not exactly. In point of fact, the thick, black lines standing on the base are drawn on the supposition that the whole height represents $1,000, and the heavy lines represent not exactly the risks at each age but the advance costs of the risks at four per cent. Thus at the age of 32 the risk of dying within a year is as 8.75 to 1,000. Hence to settle the death-claims at the end of the year, supposing interest at four per cent, each person insured at the age of 32 must pay at the beginning of the year what will amount at that rate at the end of it to $8.75 to insure $1,000, viz., $8.41. The first heavy black line at the foot of A C is intended to represent $8.41, the net cost (net because it provides for no expense but the claim) of insuring $1,000 up to the age of 33. The next heavy black line at age 33, represents $8.58, the net cost of insuring $1,000 till the age of 34, and so on. The heavy line on age 99 represents $961.54 the net cost of insuring $1,000 in the year in which the death is assumed to be certain. With these increasing net costs paid annually in advance, together with a proper addition for working expenses, the company could agree to insure the $1,000 for life, if it could only depend upon members enough continuing to pay, to constitute a fair basis of average. But looking at the dark curve of net costs of insuring a whole $1,000, growing steeper and steeper, it is easy to see that this natural method of insurance would soon come to a natural death by the healthy members ceasing to pay.

. If we apply it to a policy payable at a certain age or previous death (see Plate II.) we shall find that the costs of insuring the $1,000 at each age are just the same as before, till the last year, when as the claim is certainly to be paid at the end of that year, $961.54 must be paid at the beginning of it. This sort of endowment, is of course too steep for practice.

Now, let us return to the long policy, payable at 100 or previous death (by the assumption used in determining the premium) and consider the long ago discovered method of

getting over this difficulty, by substituting for the ever increasing net costs of insuring $1,000 an equivalent constant
net premium. Postponing for the present the question how
this equivalent constant premium is ascertained, we will take
it for granted that it has been, and see what its effect will
be.

At the age of 32 the constant net annual premium equivalent to the increasing series of net costs, standing on A B
(Plate I.) is $18.04, represented by A P on the perpendicular
A C. It seems hardly possible that this can be so, and history as well as the judgment of the eye would seem to
contradict it. But history would have had nothing to say,
if the companies had always taken proper care of the difference between the $18.04 and the $8.41 (or rather $8.33),
instead of squandering it in needless expenses.

Let us suppose the company to consist of 84,831 members. (See scale of Living and Dying in Appendix.) It is
plain that if each paid $18.04 instead of $8.41, the 742 who
die the first year would pay in advance towards their own
claims 742 times $9.63, or $7,145.46, more than on the other
plan. This would be so much saved to the other 84,089
members and would be about 8½ cents each, so that their
insurance would cost them only about $8.32½ instead of
$8.41. Consequently the company would have on hand from
each member $18.04—$8.32½=$9.71½ as reserve, which at
the end of the year at four per cent. would amount to·
$10.10. Let a star be placed on the second perpendicular
which marks the age 33, so that the portion of it intercepted between the star and the base shall be to the whole
of it as $10.10 to $1,000. Plainly the company's risk this
first year has not been $1,000, as it would have been if only
$8.41 had been paid, but $1,000—$10.10=$989.90. For as
$1,000 is to $8.41 so is $989.90 to $8.32½, or $8.33, to write
to the nearest cent, the cost of the insurance as we have
already seen. Again, at the end of the second year the

reserve from another difference and the former one will have accumulated to $20.53, which is marked by a star on the perpendicular at the age 34, and of course the company's risk the second year will be but $979.47. And as $1,000 is to $8.58 so is $979.47 to $8.40, the cost of the insurance the second year.

In this way, by letting the lines intercepted between the stars on the perpendiculars and the base represent the reserves that arise from funding the excesses of the net constant premium over the costs of insurance, we have the $1,000 always divided into the risk borne by the company, which in case of a claim is to be made up out of the costs of insurance of the surviving members, and the risk borne by the party himself, which is wholly paid out of the reserve or fund arising from his past payments beyond the cost of insurance. The effect of substituting for the natural increasing scale of premiums the equivalent constant premium is to restrict the company's risks—*if it reserves properly*—to the decreasing series of lines intercepted between the stars and the line C D, while the increasing series of lines between the stars and the base is the domain of the self-insurance or savings bank. The annual advance cost of the insurances done by the company are laid off as dark lines downward from the top of the parallelogram, and they always bear the same ratio to the part of the coinciding perpendicular above the star, that the dark line at the base does to the whole. If we lay off the constant net premium $18.04 from top C P' and draw a line through P' parallel to the top, we shall easily see how the series of constant premiums, C P', is equivalent to the risks actually borne by the company, for it exceeds the cost of the insurance for thirty years. Thus the first rash judgment of the eye is corrected. But everything depends upon the integrity of the reserve. Should this not be maintained, we can see by comparing the constant net premium with the increasing ones for the whole sum, as represented at the base of the parallelogram, that it very soon becomes insufficient to carry the risk of the whole $1,000.

The policy represented in the diagram on Plate I. of which the analysis is given in a subsequent note, is usually called a *whole-life* policy, though in regard to its premium and reserve, it is in reality an endowment insurance policy payable at the age of 100 or previous death. With a very slight enhancement of the premium it could be made payable at 75 or previous death. Really the constant net annual premium (let this be taken for granted at present) is only $19.05. (See Table No. 2 for a complete analysis of this policy.) Turn to Plate II. Fig. 1, and we shall see the heavy lines representing the net costs of insuring $1,000, on the natural method, the same, as far as the policy goes, as in the long policy of Plate I. The stars placed on the perpendiculars to represent the height at successive ages of the series of reserves (Table No. 2), here rise a little more rapidly than in the former case, thus so much more reducing the risks borne by the company that the series of " normal costs of insurance " (insurance done by the company) and represented by the series of heavy lines at the top of the parallelogram is much smaller. This leaves a larger part of the net premium to be deposited in the savings bank.

As has been already and cannot be too often remarked, a policy payable at 75 or previous death ought to be regarded as a whole-life policy, because it covers the whole of life which is, as a general rule, insurable. The extravagant risks which come after that age, no matter how much reduced in magnitude by the reserve, have commonly no insurable interest to justify them. And the policy would almost never be kept up beyond that age, if an equitable surrender value could be obtained for it.

If we consider in the same way the policy payable at 45 or previous death (Plate II., Fig. 2), which is fully analyzed in

Table No. 3, we shall find a still more remarkable diminution of the insurance done by the company, and increase of the self-insurance or savings-bank element. Here the constant net premium equivalent to all the net costs of insuring $1,000, represented by the heavy perpendiculars on the base will be $62.87; and it may be worth while now to consider how this is ascertained, because in this case the calculation is the same in method, though not so tedious in its extent, as in the others.

The present value of a dollar to be paid a certain number of years hence,—say ten years,—provided a person now aged 32 is then living, depends upon two things: the interest of money and the probability at that age of living ten years. If life were certain, it would be simply a dollar discounted at compound interest for ten years, which at four per cent. would be about 67½ cents; or more precisely, .675564. But the probability at 32 of living ten years (see Rate of Mortality in the Appendix) is expressed by the ratio of the number living by the scale at 42 to the number living at 32, thus: 77012/84831; so that the present value of a dollar, at 4 per cent., when contingent on the chance of a person aged 32 being alive to pay it at the end of ten years, is 77012/84831 of $0.675564, which is about $0.6133. In the following table, column A gives the present values of a dollar, found in this way, to be paid in each of the 13 years of the term, *if the party is alive to pay it*, beginning with the $1 paid at the start. The sum of these values is $9.8692. Column B gives the advance net costs of insuring $1,000, as laid down in the short, heavy perpendiculars on the base, together with the tall one of the beginning of the last year—the premiums of the natural method. Each dollar in this column, B, referred back to the start, is worth the portion of a dollar standing against it in column A. Hence, multiplying the values in B by the fractions in A, gives the values at the start of all the natural premiums in B; and their sum is $620.44. This, on the two assumptions

5

of mortality and interest, is the sum which, paid at the start, would be precisely equivalent to all the natural premiums of B, considering separately the chances of the party being alive to pay them when due. Now as $9.8692 is to $1, so is $620.44 to $62.866, the equivalent constant net annual premium to insure $1,000, payable at 45 or previous death.

AGE.	A	B	C	D	E
32, ...	1.	8.41	8.41	7.93	7.93
33, ...	.9531	8.58	8.18	7.57	7.22
34, ...	.9083	8.75	7.95	7.18	6.52
35, ...	.8654	8.93	7.73	6.74	5.84
36, ...	.8244	9.12	7.52	6.26	5.16
37, ...	.7852	9.31	7.31	5.72	4.49
38, ...	.7477	9.53	7.13	5.13	3.84
39, . . . ,	.7118	9.74	6.93	4.48	3.19
40, ...	.6775	9.96	6.75	3.75	2.54
41, ...	.6447	10.20	6.58	2.95	1·90
42, ...	.6133	10.48	6.43	2.07	1.27
43, ...	.5833	10.82	6.31	1.10	.64
44, ...	.5545	961.54	533.21	–	. –
.	9.8692		620.44		50.54

It is essential in every such calculation, where compound interest is concerned, to treat every payment *separately*, as in the case above cited. Hence the tediousness of the process, when the possible payments are very numerous, unless resort is had to abridged methods, in which the reasons are concealed.

Now having ascertained the constant net annual premium equivalent to the natural ones in this short " endowment insurance," as it is called, we shall find that those we assumed in the other cases can be found in the same way; and the three cases differ from each other in no respect whatever, except in the different ratios of the insurance to the self-insurance. In the first case, where the term was 68 years, and the constant net annual premium $18.04, the reserve increases so that the company's risks are the black lines at the top, instead of those at the bottom. But on account of the enormous risks of the years beyond 75, even the lines at the top become at length more than twice as large as the constant net premium, so that they absorb the whole of it, and a part of the interest on the reserve. In other words, the annual deposit in the savings bank becomes *negative* (see Table No. 1 in the note), so that the curve of stars denoting the height of the reserve, which began by increasing so rapidly as to have its concavity upward, slackens its rate of increase and turns its concavity downwards from about 75. Cutting off these enormous risks and closing the policy at 75, has the effect of so diminishing the company's risks that no part of the interest on the reserve (unless the entry is at a very early age) is in any year required to meet the normal costs of carrying those risks, as is plain enough from the diagram (Plate II. Fig. 1) and from the Table No. 2. Hence with the very slight increase of the constant net premium from $18.04 to $19.05, the reserve amounts to the whole sum insured in 43 years.

In case the policy is closed at 45 (Table No. 3, and Plate II. Fig. 2), the great preponderance of the self-insurance has the effect of making the insurance done by the company almost incredibly small, as represented by the stubby little dark lines at the top of the parallelogram. If we ascertain the value of these insurances by the company at the start, we shall find that less than one of the net premiums ($62.87) will pay for the whole of them. This may be easily done by recurring to the foregoing table, where column D gives the normal costs of these successive company's risks. If they are all referred to the start, by multiplying each by the corresponding present value of a dollar in column A, we shall have in column E the present values of the whole, the sum of which is $50.54, which may be called the insurance value of the policy. We have already found that the single advance

net premium, equivalent to the whole of 'the natural ones, is
$620.44. If we subtract from this the $50.54, we shall have
$569.90 as the advance value of the self-insurance or savings-
bank business on the policy. Thus we see that in this policy
the savings-bank or self-insurance element is a little more
than eleven times as great as the insurance element. If we
apply a similar calculation to the policy payable at death or
75, we shall find that the advance cost of the insurance to be
done by the company is $174.70, and of that to be done by the
party himself is $156.50. Here the savings-bank element is
not so great as the insurance element by more than ten per
cent. In the policy payable at death or 100, the advance
value of the insurance element will be found to be $204.42,
while that of the savings-bank element is only $114.89; or a
little more than one-third of the whole.

It seems quite obvious from these considerations, that if a
company consists of policies having so wide a variety in
regard to the proportion in which these two elements enter
into them, it must be quite necessary to equity that the two
elements should be kept distinct, and that while the insurance
part of the business is managed on correct insurance principles, the savings-bank part of the business—just so far as it is
such—should be managed on savings-bank principles. This
is the aim of these tables.

Though prepared with a good deal of care, they undoubtedly contain a multitude of errors, which seem to have a fatal
facility of creeping into such a work. It is hoped, however,
that most of them are so small that if laid off on the diagrams
we have been explaining they would not be perceptible to
the naked eye, in which case they will not be of great practical damage.

There is added in a note (Table No. 1) a full analysis of
the policy illustrated in Plate I., for the sake of showing why
it should never be sought for or issued. This must be obvious to any one who carefully compares this table with Table

No. 2, or with any of the other tables of policies issued at the same age.

The reason why policies have not heretofore been issued to any great extent with a precisely stipulated cash surrender value is that there has been no great public demand for them. And there has been no such demand because the public did not well understand the most desirable, convenient and equitable form of life insurance. Our companies are numerous, and all of them ready to accommodate the public with almost every conceivable form of policy, often making concessions much more inconvenient if not hazardous to the company than any proposed in these savings-bank insurance policies. If any healthy and insurable person should offer to any company to take any one of these 268 policies, with surrender value stipulated according to the last column of the table, it must be uncommonly dull in its appetite for business or obtuse in its perception of its own interests to decline.

The greater part of our life-insurance companies, including some of the most prosperous and useful, have indulged the public in a concession much less conservative than that of stipulating the cash surrender value proposed, to wit, that of taking a considerable part of the premium in notes from the start. If the surrender value stated in the last column of these tables is all that can be fairly conceded with such premiums, then, plainly, no part of the premium should be taken in notes till the year at the end of which there is a sur-. render value, and then not beyond such value. Against this surrender value the note, of course, is as good an asset to the company as any other. Beyond this, it is hazardous or doubtful.

The premium note, as has been already remarked, and as everybody knows, is in effect a surrender value stipulated, for in case of discontinuance it is never collected. In regard to justice and fair dealing it is sometimes too much and sometimes too little. In regard to equity between part-note payers and all-cash payers, there can be none unless the latter are paid, when they discontinue, as much cash as the former are paid notes, when the reserve is the same. There has never existed any rule to this effect. The notes are a source of great disappointment to simple-minded policyholders. They should only be resorted to in an emergency to tide the policy over a shallow place in a man's income. Resorted to from the start they have the effect of substituting for a constant premium, securing a fixed sum to the widow, an increasing premium securing a diminishing sum. A terrible deception is practised upon the public in making people believe that the surplus will so far wipe out the notes, as to make the policy as good as one paid for in cash. If this were true, a man might become rich by depositing his notes in a savings bank. The only cases where a premium-note policy is as good as one paid for in cash, are, first, when the party can get more interest on the deposit part of his premium out of the company than in it, and second, when he wishes to discontinue and the company will not give a cash surrender value equal to the note. If he gives for a policy all the cash he can spare and a note besides, he runs a serious risk of being obliged to relinquish his policy when he needs to keep it up.

The savings-bank insurance, with stipulated cash surrender value, and margins adjusted to an equitable assessment of expenses, gives a person the best possible chance of getting all the insurance he needs at a fair cost, *without being obliged ever to pay for more than he needs.* Under the present non-forfeiture plans, whether secured by stipulation or legislation, the person who becomes unable or unwilling to pay further premiums, gets as his surrender value only some more insurance. This is better than nothing, but *may* not be so good as the money. For an obvious reason the company cannot pay money or insurance at the option of the party at the time of discontinuance, though it might have stipulated either the one or the other at his option declared at the start. But if the party gets the cash surrender value stipulated at the start, he is all right in any event. For, taking the example in Table No. 2, suppose he has paid ten premiums and finds himself unable to pay the eleventh. If he has ceased to need further insurance he receives $101.79 in cash; he would have received not more than $60 or $80 if it had not been stipulated in the policy. If he does need further insurance and is in good health, the company will doubtless lend him a premium or two on the security of his surrender value, rather than have the policy drop. But suppose his health is bad, so that the company had rather pay the $101.79 and have the policy drop. It is good security for that in the money market, so that the party is sure to be able to borrow on it outside of the company to keep it in force. Thus, provided he needs the insurance, he can by means of the cash surrender value stipulation, oblige the company to furnish it to the extent of $88\frac{1}{10}$ per cent. of his reserve. Under the present Massachusetts law to regulate the forfeiture of policies he can get further insurance only to the extent of 80 per cent. of his reserve, whatever it may be. Under this law, of course, he fares a little better, as to further insurance, when the reserve is quite small. But it fails in a great measure to protect him, in that respect, when his reserve is large, and altogether when he needs the money more than the insurance.

The reader, it is to be hoped, if he has a family dependent on his earnings, will not fail to take one more look at these diagrams, and by noticing how small an annual payment creates a fortune to leave behind him, become impressed with the manly resolution to lose no time in securing one.

NOTE.—The following is a complete analysis (illustrated in Plate I.) of what is called the "ordinary whole-life policy," but which is really a policy for $1,000 payable at DEATH or 100.

TABLE No. 1.

Age of entry 32. Gross Premium $24.10. Net Premium $18.04.

Age of Person	Insurance					Self-Insurance			Age of Policy
	Margin	Normal Costs of Insurance	Company's Risks	Insurance Values	Surrender Charges	Deposits	Reserve	Surrender Values	
32	$6 06	$8 33	$989 90	$204 42	-	$9 71	-	-	0
33	6 08	8 40	979 47	205 74	$16 46	9 64	$10 10	00	1
34	6 06	8 47	968 70	207 08	16 56	9 57	20 53	$3 97	2
35	6 08	8 55	957 58	208 45	16 68	9 49	31 30	14 62	3
36	6 06	8 63	946 10	209 84	16 79	9 41	42 42	25 63	4
37	6 08	8 70	934 23	211 26	16 90	9 34	53 90	37 00	5
38	6 06	8 78	921 97	212 73	17 02	9 26	65 77	48 75	6
39	6 06	8 86	909 30	214 22	17 14	9 18	78 03	60 89	7
40	8 08	8 93	896 20	215 77	17 28	9 11	90 70	73 44	8
41	6 06	9 01	882 66	217 37	17 39	9 03	103 80	86 41	9
42	8 08	9 10	868 67	219 02	17 52	8 94	117 34	99 82	10
43	6 06	9 24	854 26	220 72	17 66	8 80	131 33	113 67	11
44	8 08	9 44	839 48	222 44	17 79	8 80	145 74	127 95	12
45	6 06	9 68	824 36	224 14	17 93	8 36	160 62	142 69	13
46	8 06	9 98	808 95	225 80	18 08	8 06	175 64	157 68	14

Age			
15	$172 87	$191 05	$7 95
16	188 43	206 73	7 38
17	204 27	222 68	7 02
18	220 38	238 89	6 63
19	236 74	255 34	6 21
20	253 34	272 01	5 77
21	270 17	288 90	5 30
22	287 19	305 97	4 82
23	304 40	323 22	4 30
24	321 79	340 62	3 77
25	339 33	358 17	3 23
26	357 04	375 86	2 66
27	374 87	393 66	2 06
28	392 81	411 55	1 40
29	410 80	429 47	71
30	428 80	447 39	02
31	446 79	465 27	—77
32	464 73	483 08	—1 56
33	482 59	500 78	—2 37
34	500 34	518 35	—3 22
35	517 93	535 74	—4 09
36	535 33	552 92	—4 97
37	552 52	569 87	—5 85
38	569 50	586 58	—6 75
39	586 23	603 02	—7 65

Age					
47	$18 18	$227 36	$793 27	$10 09	$6 06
48	18 30	228 83	777 32	10 66	6 06
49	18 41	230 18	761 11	11 02	6 06
50	18 51	231 40	744 66	11 41	6 06
51	18 60	232 50	727 99	11 83	6 06
52	18 67	233 44	711 10	12 27	6 06
53	18 73	234 22	694 03	12 74	6 06
54	18 78	234 83	676 78	13 22	6 06
55	18 82	235 25	659 38	13 74	6 06
56	18 83	235 48	641 83	14 27	6 06
57	18 84	235 50	624 14	14 81	6 06
58	18 82	235 33	606 34	15 38	6 06
59	18 79	234 94	499 65	15 98	6 06
60	18 74	234 33	481 65	16 64	6 06
61	18 67	233 48	464 26	17 33	6 06
62	18 59	232 37	447 08	18 06	6 06
63	18 48	231 00	430 13	18 81	6 06
64	18 35	229 36	413 42	19 60	6 06
65	18 19	227 46	396 98	20 41	6 06
66	18 01	225 23	380 82	21 26	6 06
67	17 81	222 74	447 08	22 13	6 06
68	17 59	219 96	430 13	23 01	6 06
69	17 35	216 90	413 42	23 89	6 06
70	17 08	213 56	396 98	24 79	6 06
71	16 79	209 95	380 82	25 69	6 06

6*

TABLE No. 1—Continued.

Age of entry 32. Gross Premium $24.10. Net Premium $18.04.

Age of Policy	Self-Insurance			Surrender Charges.	Insurance			Margin.	Age of Person.
	Surrender Values.	Reserve.	Deposits.		Insurance Values.	Company's Risks.	Normal Costs of Insurance.		
40	$602 70	$619 18	—$8 56	$16 48	$206 09	$364	$26 60	$6 06	72
41	618 88	635 04	—9 47	16 16	201 97	349 41	27 51	6 06	73
42	634 78	650 59	—10 39	15 81	197 62	334 19	28 43	6 06	74
43	650 37	665 81	—11 30	15 44	193 03	319 31	29 34	6 06	75
44	665 63	680 69	—12 20	15 06	188 23	304 77	30 24	6 06	76
45	680 58	695 23	—13 10	14 65	183 22	290 58	31 14	6 06	77
46	695 18	709 42	—14 02	14 24	177 99	276 78	32 06	6 06	78
47	709 42	723 22	—14 89	13 80	172 56	263 34	32 93	6 06	79
48	723 31	736 66	—15 75	13 35	166 93	250 25	33 79	6 06	80
49	736 87	749 75	—16 54	12 88	161 09	237 46	34 58	6 06	81
50	750 14	762 54	—17 25	12 40	155 06	224 90	35 29	6 06	82
51	763 20	775 10	—17 91	11 90	148 85	212 52	35 95	6 06	83
52	776 18	787 48	—18 48	11 30	142 48	200 24	36 52	6 06	84
53	788 88	799 76	—19 04	10 88	136 00	188 05	37 08	6 08	85
54	801 60	811 95	—19 60	10 35	129 42	175 95	37 64	6 06	86
55	814 23	824 05	—20 14	9 82	122 77	163 93	38 18	6 06	87
56	826 78	836 07	—20 74	9 29	116 09	152 06	38 78	6 06	88
57	839 18	847 94	—21 44	8 76	109 44	140 44	39 48	6 06	89

Age									Age
58	$861 33	$869 58	$22 14	$8 23	$102 83	$129 08	$40 18	$6 06	90
59	863 21	870 92	—22 95	7 71	98 37	118 11	40 99	6 06	91
60	874 68	881 89	—23 94	7 21	90 11	107 73	41 98	6 06	92
61	885 54	892 27	—25 10	6 73	84 18	98 14	43 14	6 06	93
62	895 57	901 86	—26 40	6 29	78 65	89 52	44 44	6 06	94
63	904 60	910 48	—28 36	5 88	73 57	82 60	46 40	6 06	95
64	911 96	917 40	—30 13	5 44	67 99	77 24	48 17	6 06	96
65	918 06	922 76	—26 61	4 70	58 74	70 08	46 65	6 06	97
66	926 66	929 92	—22 71	3 26	40 75	56 50	40 75	6 06	98
67	943 50	943 50	—18 04	3 00	40 75	56 50	40 75	6 06	99
68	1000 00	1000 00		0 00	0 00	0 00	0 00	0 00	100

TABLE No. 2.—DEATH OR 75.

* Age of entry 32.   Gross Premium $26.71.   Net Premium $19.05.

Age of Person.	Margin.	Normal Costs of Insurance.	Company's Risks.	Insurance Values.	Surrender Charges.	Deposits.	Reserve.	Surrender Values.	Age of Policy.
	Insurance.					Self-Insurance.			
32	$7 66	$8 32	$988 84	$174 70	—	$10 73	—	—	0
33	7 66	8 38	977 30	174 60	$13 97	10 67	$11 16	00	1
34	7 66	8 44	965 34	174 40	13 95	10 61	22 70	$8 75	2
35	7 66	8 52	952 99	174 15	13 93	10 53	34 66	20 73	3
36	7 66	8 58	940 21	173 88	13 91	10 47	47 01	33 10	4
37	7 66	8 64	927 01	173 59	13 89	10 41	59 79	45 90	5
38	7 66	8 70	913 32	173 20	13 86	10 35	72 99	59 13	6
39	7 66	8 76	899 16	172 79	13 82	10 29	86 68	72 86	7
40	7 66	8 82	884 46	172 34	13 79	10 23	100 84	87 05	8
41	7 66	8 87	869 25	171 88	13 75	10 18	115 54	101 79	9
42	7 66	8 94	853 51	171 35	13 71	10 11	130 75	117 04	10
43	7 66	9 07	837 25	170 72	13 66	9 98	146 49	132 83	11
44	7 66	9 23	820 53	170 10	13 61	9 82	162 75	149 14	12
45	7 66	9 43	803 33	169 24	13 54	9 62	179 47	165 93	13
46	7 66	9 70	785 75	168 25	13 46	9 35	196 67	183 21	14
47	7 66	9 98	767 74	167 05	13 37	9 07	214 25	200 88	15
48	7 66	10 27	749 33	165 61	13 25	8 78	232 26	219 01	16
49	7 66	10 58	730 48	163 88	13 11	8 47	250 67	237 66	17

Age	A	B	C	D	E	F	G	H	Age
18	$258 57	$269 52	$8 15	$12 96	$161 86	$711 23	$10 90	$7 66	50
19	276 99	288 77	7 81	12 76	159 51	691 66	11 24	7 66	51
20	295 89	308 44	7 46	12 55	156 85	671 45	11 59	7 66	52
21	316 24	328 55	7 10	12 31	153 81	650 92	11 95	7 66	53
22	337 05	349 08	6 74	12 03	150 42	629 94	12 31	7 66	54
23	358 33	370 06	6 38	11 73	146 69	608 51	12 67	7 66	55
24	380 10	391 49	6 00	11 39	142 35	586 60	13 05	7 66	56
25	402 39	413 40	5 66	11 01	137 70	564 17	13 39	7 66	57
26	425 22	435 83	5 32	10 61	132 60	541 20	13 73	7 66	58
27	448 64	458 80	4 99	10 16	126 95	517 66	14 06	7 66	59
28	472 67	482 34	4 66	9 67	120 84	493 52	14 39	7 66	60
29	497 35	506 48	4 35	9 13	144 12	468 74	14 70	7 66	61
30	522 71	531 26	4 08	8 55	106 87	443 23	14 97	7 66	62
31	548 85	556 77	3 88	7 92	99 04	416 93	15 17	7 66	63
32	575 81	583 07	3 75	7 26	90 72	389 71	15 30	7 66	64
33	603 75	610 29	3 73	6 54	81 80	361 41	15 32	7 66	65
34	632 81	638 59	3 86	5 78	72 30	331 84	15 19	7 66	66
35	683 17	868 16	4 16	4 99	62 34	300 80	14 89	7 66	67
36	695 04	699 20	4 72	4 16	52 06	267 92	14 33	7 66	68
37	728 76	732 08	5 60	3 32	41 53	232 81	13 45	7 66	69
38	764 70	767 19	8 68	2 49	31 06	194 96	12 17	7 66	70
39	803 36	805 04	8 68	1 68	21 03	153 74	10 37	7 66	71
40	845 31	846 26	11 16	95	11 92	108 29	7 89	7 66	72
41	891 35	891 71	14 52	36	4 53	57 51	4 53	7 66	73
42	942 49	942 49	19 05	00	00	00	00	7 66	74
43	1000 00	1000 00	–	–	–	–	–	–	75

TABLE No. 3.—DEATH OR 45.

Age of entry 32.   Gross Premium $66.55.   Net Premium $62.87.

Age of Person.	Margin.	Insurance.				Self-Insurance.			Age of Policy.
		Normal Costs of Insurance.	Company's Risks.	Insurance Values.	Surrender Charges.	Deposits.	Reserve.	Surrender Values.	
32	$3 68	$7 93	$945 86	$50 55	—	$54 94	—	—	0
33	3 68	7 57	883 08	44 70	$3 58	55 30	$57 14	$53 58	1
34	3 68	7 18	820 49	38 97	3 12	55 69	116 92	113 80	2
35	3 68	6 74	754 93	33 36	2 67	56 13	179 51	176 84	3
36	3 68	6 26	686 25	27 94	2 24	56 61	245 07	242 83	4
37	3 68	5 72	614 30	22 77	1 82	57 15	313 75	311 93	5
38	3 68	5 13	538 82	17 90	1 43	57 74	385 70	384 27	6
39	3 68	4 48	459 65	13 41	1 07	58 39	461 18	460 11	7
40	3 68	3 75	376 56	9 38	75	59 12	540 35	539 60	8
41	3 68	2 95	289 31	5 91	47	59 92	623 44	622 97	9
42	3 68	2 07	197 66	3 11	25	60 80	710 69	710 44	10
43	3 68	1 10	101 33	1 10	09	61 77	802 34	802 25	11
44	3 68	00	00	00	00	62 87	898 67	898 67	12
45	—	—	—	—	—	—	1000 00	1000 00	13

TABLE No. 4.—DEATH OR 50.

Age of entry 25. Gross Premium $32.91. Net Premium $28.88.

| Age of Person. | Margin. | Normal Costs of Insurance. | Insurance | | | Self-Insurance | | | Age of Policy. |
			Company's Risks.	Insurance Values.	Surrender Charges.	Deposits.	Reserve.	Surrender Values.	
25	$4 23	$7 30	$977 75	$85 14	—	$21 38	—	—	0
26	4 23	7 24	954 55	81 57	$6 53	21 44	$22 25	$15 72	1
27	4 23	7 16	930 36	77 95	6 24	21 52	45 45	39 21	2
28	4 23	7 08	905 10	74 19	5 94	21 60	69 64	63 70	3
29	4 23	6 99	878 75	70 36	5 63	21 69	94 90	89 27	4
30	4 23	6 90	851 24	66 47	5 32	21 78	121 25	115 93	5
31	4 23	6 79	822 51	62 47	5 00	21 89	148 76	143 76	6
32	4 23	6 67	792 51	58 42	4 67	22 01	177 49	172 82	7
33	4 23	6 58	761 17	54 30	4 34	22 15	207 49	203 15	8
34	4 23	6 37	728 41	50 14	4 01	22 31	238 83	234 82	9
35	4 23	6 20	694 15	45 94	3 67	22 48	271 59	267 92	10
36	4 23	6 00	658 31	41 71	3 34	22 68	305 85	302 51	11
37	4 23	5 78	620 86	37 50	3 00	22 90	341 69	338 69	12
38	4 23	5 54	581 62	33 31	2 66	23 14	379 14	376 48	13
39	4 23	5 27	540 52	29 16	2 33	23 41	418 38	416 05	14

Table No. 4.—Concluded.

Age of entry 25.   Gross Premium $32.91.   Net Premium $28.68.

Age of Person.	Insurance.					Self-Insurance.			Age of Policy.
	Margin.	Normal Costs of Insurance.	Company's Risks.	Insurance Values.	Surrender Charges.	Deposits.	Reserve.	Surrender Value.	
40	$4 23	$4 96	$497 47	$25 11	$2 01	$23 72	$459 48	$457 47	15
41	4 23	4 62	452 33	21 18	1 69	24 06	502 53	500 84	16
42	4 23	4 24	405 03	17 41	1 39	24 44	547 67	546 28	17
43	4 23	3 84	355 37	13 85	1 11	24 84	594 97	593 86	18
44	4 23	3 41	303 30	10 52	84	25 27	644 63	643 79	19
45	4 23	2 92	248 64	7 48	60	25 76	696 70	696 10	20
46	4 23	2 36	191 21	4 80	38	26 32	761 36	750 98	21
47	4 23	1 70	130 79	2 67	21	26 98	808 79	808 58	22
48	4 23	92	67 15	92	07	27 76	869 21	869 14	23
49	4 23	00	00	00	00	28 68	932 85	932 85	24
50	—	—	—	—	—	—	1000 00	1000 00	25

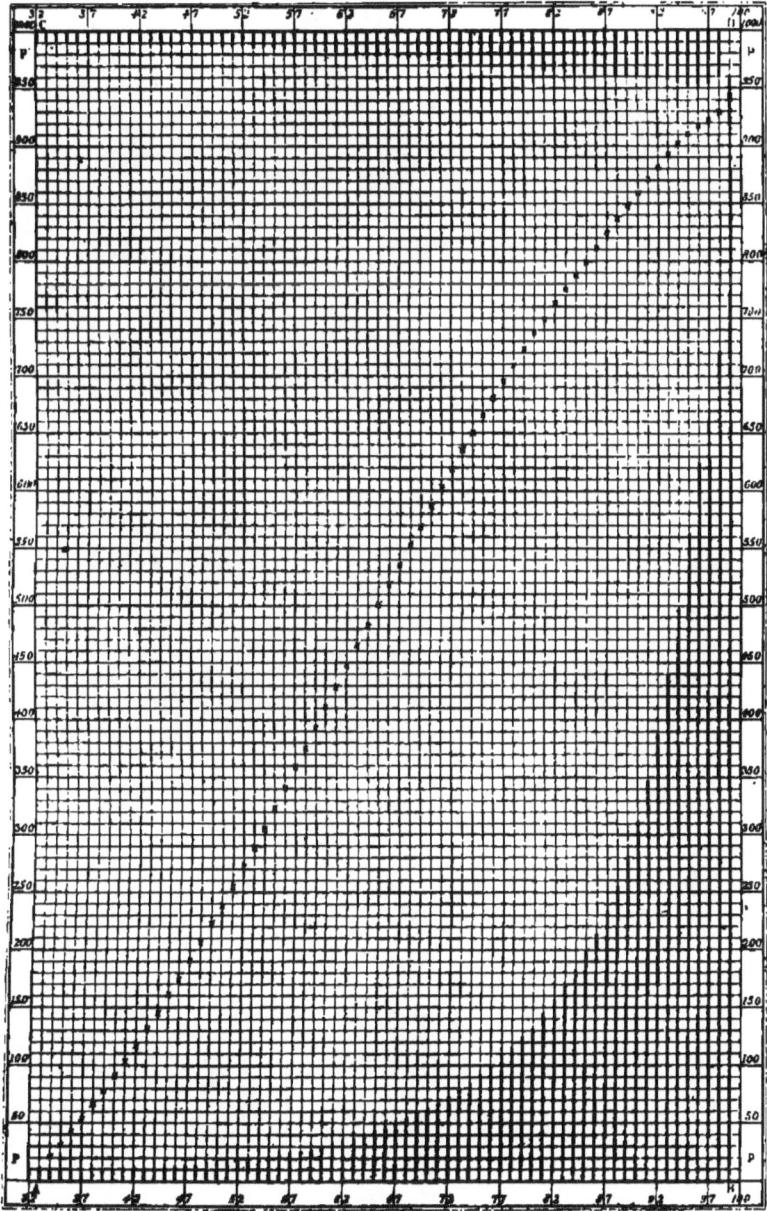

Plate 1

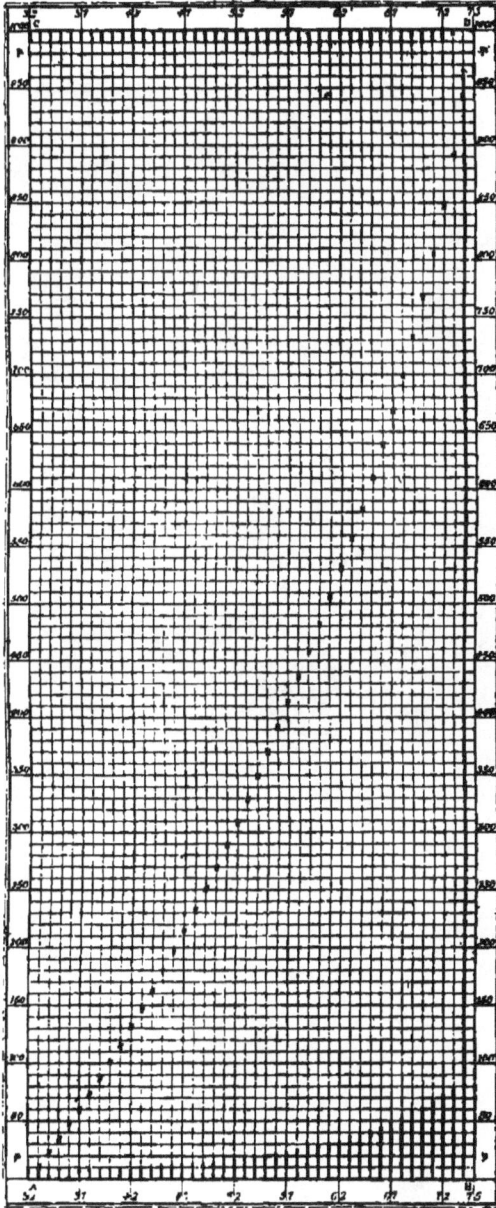

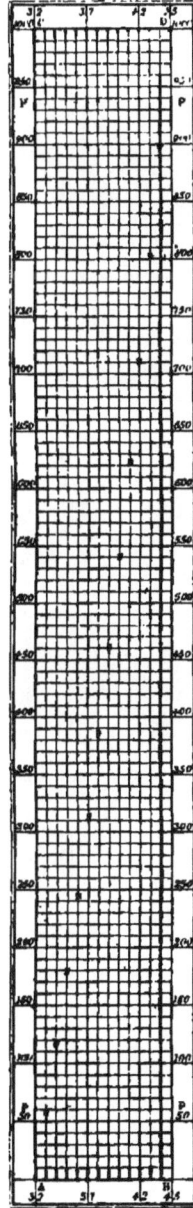

Plate II.

Fig. I.

Fig. II.

With the exception of short-term policies, which are frequently of great convenience, no others are really required besides such as may be fully pre-calculated in two or three hundred tables like Nos. 2, 3 and 4 above. For example, a joint policy is never necessary, for if two persons are insurable and wish to insure for each other's benefit, the premium which would be paid for the joint policy, payable to the survivor on the death of either, may be divided between two policies, one on each life. Then when one becomes a claim, the other may be surrendered, and the survivor will be as much bene-fited as if the policy had been that present pest of the offices, a joint one. This arrangement would naturally lead the officers to look after the insura-ble interest of each party in the other, instead of contenting themselves, as at present, with finding *one* insurable interest for the *two* risks.

These Savings Bank Insurance Tables are offered to the public as a practical solution of the impor-tant problem, how to conduct the business and ad-just the premiums of long and short term endow-ment insurances, so that no one can afford to put the difference between the premiums of the two for the same amount at the same age in a pure savings bank, and take the longer term in the insurance company; in other words, how to make the increase of the *self-insurance* on a given policy diminish the cost of the *insurance by the company*,

instead of increasing it as is now the case. Under
the old system, the increase of the self-insurance on
a given policy diminishes the *amount* of the insurance done by the company, but enhances materially
the *cost* of what is done. The consequence of this
is, that many thrifty young people who only need
insurance for the ten or twenty years in which they
will be accumulating a competence, neglect insurance altogether and patronize the savings bank pure
and simple.

The stock, or non-participating life insurance
companies need the solution of this problem, no less
than the mutual ones. Such a company will give
a whole-life policy for $1,000 to a person aged
30, for an annual premium of $16.55, and an en-
dowment insurance, for the same amount, payable
at 40 or previous death, for an annual premium of
$87.55, a difference of $71 per annum.

Now if money is worth six per cent. per annum,
and a savings bank can be found that will accumulate it at that rate, the insured party by taking the
ten-year endowment instead of taking the whole-life
policy and putting the $71 per annum into the
savings bank, simply throws away $25.66 at the
start, even supposing that the whole-life policy at
the end of ten years, the party being then alive,
should have no value at all. To make it in any
measure expedient to take the ten-year endowment
insurance in a stock company, in preference to the

longer policy, the premium of the former must be reduced to $84.14, if not lower. If any considerable arithmetical knowledge on this subject should get afloat in this country it would be impossible for stock life insurance to flourish without adopting a savings-bank system, in which the profits of the stock shall be confined to the saving of cost on the insurance done by the company, while the self-insurance should be regarded as savings-bank deposit, withdrawable subject to a fair charge proportionate to insurance value.

Inasmuch as life insurance under a law fixing the reserve *is* a union of insurance and savings bank, and the company when issuing endowment policies *is*, in the last year of every such policy, a simple trust company, doing no insurance at all, it is not easy to see why it should not exercise savings-bank powers in any case when it is expedient. This would be a great convenience and simplification of business. Many people find it difficult to pay the whole annual premium of a policy, especially an endowment policy, at once. And this leads to splitting the premium into semi-annual, quarterly and monthly payments, a very great inconvenience to the company for reasons which it is unnecessary here to dwell on. The company can much more easily accommodate such people by deferring the issue of an insurance policy till it has received simple savings-bank deposits sufficient to pay a full

annual premium in advance. Then let any payments that can be made during the first policy year
be received as simple savings-bank deposits to be
applied with interest to the payment of the next
annual premium when it becomes due.

Chapter V.

REDUCTION OF RATES.

In the latter part of 1872 the officers of the leading Mutual Life Insurance Company proposed a
serious reduction of the premiums. This produced
a public discussion, the result of which proved that
autocracy in life insurance is far from being synony-
mous with omnipotence. Some of the incidents
and mysteries of this discussion will be noticed in
a subsequent chapter. The following letter was
intended to justify the writer's dissent from any
such reduction as that proposed :—

REPLY TO MR. WHITE.

To the Editors of the Hartford Courant.

At your invitation, the secretary of the Charter Oak Life
Insurance Company, in your issue of December 14, produces
an argument in favor of the lately proposed reduction of
rates by the Mutual Life Insurance Company of New York,
in the course of which he alludes to me in the following language : " Mr. Wright's position towards the Mutual Life is
very astonishing, when it is well known that for some time
past he has persistently urged a plan of insurance upon the
companies which, on large classes of policies, does not pro-

vide for anything like the amount of expenses which is fur-
nished by the new rates of the Mutual Life. He now objects
to a 'loading' on endowment insurances, *considerably* more
than his own plans contemplate, as being unsafe. If it is so,
what sort of an adviser is Mr. Wright to be considered when
he urges his own plans with so very little margin for expense that only one company has as yet been induced to use
them?"

He also says of me, in connection with two other persons,
that I am on record in favor of that which I now condemn.

It is not that I differ with him in regard to the reduction of
rates, or to defend myself against what I deem to be a personal injustice, but to explain a matter in which the public
has a deep interest that has thus far been left out of sight in
this discussion, that I ask space in your columns to reply to
this.

Mr. White cannot possibly be so severe on me in regard to
my past short-comings as I am on myself. But I prefer to,
tell the story of my own guilt, and confess my real crime.
It will then be seen that I am quite innocent of ever advocat-
ing *such* a reduction as the Mutual Life proposed.

Though the premiums charged by the Mutual Life Insurance Company have never, in my opinion, been, on the whole,
too high, it is quite undeniable that some of them are un-
necessarily high in relation to others. In truth there was
committed, long before I was born, and before life insurance
was born in America, a blunder in what is called "loading
the premiums," which, of course, extended to agents' commissions and the assessment of expenses among the members. This was adopted unwittingly in this country, with
most of the other rules and practices of the business. It
did not become very apparent or troublesome till we had
gone largely into the practice of issuing endowment policies.
Then, when it was attempted to distribute surplus, either on
the percentage or "contribution" plan, the most astounding

and unsatisfactory results developed themselves. I, for one, discovered that something had got wrong end foremost, but I was unable to see what, or how to set it right. I carefully explored the literature of the British Institute of Actuaries, but got no help from that. Hints of the trouble were given in the ninth Report of the Massachusetts Insurance Commissioners in 1864 (see Reports with Appendix, 1865, pages 274 and 366). By about 1869, when the blunder was cheating people out of millions, for nobody's benefit but the agents', all at once the right way of assessing expenses, compensating the agents, and keeping the accounts of a life-insurance company dawned upon me. Not to have discovered this before was intensely and almost intolerably mortifying. For nobody more heartily than I had recommended endowment insurance policies. Tens of thousands had taken them, and on the short terms had been as good as cheated, every mother's son of them. And I had ignorantly acquiesced in the stupid and stupendous blunder by which this was brought about! I could have torn the hair off from the top of my head, if there had been any there and it would have done any good. And yet I was as sure as ever that endowment policies were the right ones to take, *if they could be dealt by equitably as to their expenses.*

Nobody would have been gladder than I to have had my discovery proved a mistake. And I will pay a handsome reward to any one who will do it now. I saw then, and see now, that the companies that have trusted me as their adviser are in danger of coming to grief, not by want of funds but by want of equity within themselves. On this account I called together my brother actuaries in 1870, at the Mutual Life Office in New York, in presence of Mr. Winston, and some of his directors, and had the method of loading premiums and assessing commissions and expenses discussed. I think it was unanimously agreed by the actuaries present, that the old procedure was wrong, and the only question was how without alienating the agents, who are interested in the present exorbitant commissions on endowment policies, the base could be changed from premium to "insurance value." It was concluded that the thing was only possible by a concert of action of the leading companies, and I understood Mr. Winston to promise that he would endeavor to have a convention of the executive officers of such companies assembled for that purpose. They never assembled.

I have urged the calling of such a convention, upon several companies, with all my might. For I felt that such a blunder, affecting one of the grandest institutions of modern civilization, must be corrected. But Mr. White is not quite correct in saying that I have *urged* MY plan of doing it upon any individual company, and not at all correct when he insinuates that only one company has adopted my plan, *because* it has "so very little margin for expense." The contrary will appear by and by.

I have not *urged*, but simply offered, as a sin-offering, freely to all companies who will take it, a plan founded on equity, to which no objection has yet been offered except this: It does not in any case give or provide for, a commission to the agent larger than the company and the policy-holder himself can afford, and therefore *the agent will not work it.* The present fact is, that on any other plan in any company, the agent gets a larger commission just about in the ratio that the policy is worth less to the company, and so large on short terms that no man but a fool or a dupe *ever* takes one. Why, will be plainer by and by.

The ordinary mind commonly fails to understand the subject I am talking about, because the law of human mortality extends over so many years and is complicated with compound interest. The equities would be just the same in kind if life were shorter and money yielded no interest. Hence the easiest way to understand them will be to take a hypothetical law of mortality, confined to a very small number of years, and suppose the rate of interest zero. Let us, for example, suppose that life could last at longest but *four* years, and that one out of four will die the first year, one out of three the second, one out of two the third, and the rest in the fourth year. This law of mortality is expressed by the series $\frac{1}{4}, \frac{1}{3}, \frac{1}{2}, \frac{1}{1}$. Now if we take a mutual life insurance company of four members, all entering in the first year of age, each insuring for $1,000, the normal or natural net premiums will be as follows:—

1st year, ...	$250 00
2d year, ...	333 33
3d year, ...	500 00
4th year, ...	1,000 00

This increasing series of premiums would be objectionable, for reasons too obvious to mention. How can we make the premiums constant or level? Obviously as much must be paid one way as the other to meet the aggregate of death-claims, which will be $4,000. Of the level premiums, whatever they may be, there will be four paid the first year, three the second, two the third and one the last,—in all, ten,—so that each must be $400. This will give the company $600 the first year beyond the one death-claim and of course it must be held in reserve for the future. The three premiums paid the second year will leave $200 to be added to the reserve from the first, making it $800. The income of the third year will be $800, making it necessary to take $200 from the reserve, thus leaving it $600, which with the $400 received the fourth year will pay the last death-claim, and would just as well pay it, if the man should continue to live, in violation of the law. As to the premiums and necessary reserve from each, under this law, it would make no difference whether the number entering the first year were four or more. Each living member must then have a reserve, as follows : at the end of the

1st year,	. . . .	$200	00
2d year,	. . . . . .	400	00
3d year,	. . . . . .	600	00
4th year,	. . . .	1,000	00

This is as much as to say, the party paying $400 the first year, compared with one paying the normal premium of $250 for $1,000 of insurance from the company, really *insures himself* for $200, and the company only insures him the complementary $800 at the normal premium of ¼ or $200. The next year he *insures himself* $400 and pays the company the normal rate of ⅖, or $200, for carrying the complementary risk of $600. The third year he *insures himself* $600, and pays the company the normal rate of ½ or $200, for carrying the complementary risk of $400. The last year he *insures himself* the whole $1,000, for if there were any number of living members, entered subsequently, not one of them would have to contribute a dime to his claim. And let it be observed that the *reserve* of a living member never has to be touched to pay the claim of a dead one. That is always made up out of the normal insurance premiums of himself and the living members that year, *and his own* reserve, or *self-insurance.* This is a financial necessity of substituting a constant or level premium for the natural increasing premium, which admits no reserve out of the net premium. It does not become any less a necessity if legislation steps in and compels it.

Under such a statute, at any rate, the contract naturally resolves itself into two things, very distinct in kind, and which cannot be confounded or left mixed up, when policies of different terms and conditions are issued, without making the wildest work with equity.

Distinguishing the successive self-insurances from the insurance by the company, we have under the level premium the two following series :—

7

YEAR.	SELF-INSURANCE.		INSURED BY COMPANY.	
	Deposit.	Sum.	Premium.	Sum.
1, ...	$200 00	$200 00	$200 00	$800 00
2, ...	200 00	400 00	200 00	600 00
3, ...	200 00	600 00	200 00	400 00
4, ...	400 00	1000 00	–	–

This is a whole-life policy on our miniature mortality table, without interest or expense. Let us see how it would be on the same hypothesis with a three-year endowment insurance, which would be calculated just as if two instead of one died in the third year. Then there would be only nine of the net level premiums to meet $4,000, and of course each would be $444.44 about, and the contract would resolve itself into two, as follows:—

YEAR.	SELF-INSURANCE.		INSURED BY COMPANY.	
	Deposit.	Sum.	Premium.	Sum.
1, . . .	$259 25	$259 25	$185 19	$740 75
2, . . .	296 29	555 54	148 15	444 46
3, . . .	444 44	1000 00	–	–

If it were a two-year endowment insurance, the net premium would, in the same way, be found to be $571.43. And the contract would resolve itself into two, as follows:—

YEAR.	SELF-INSURANCE.		INSURED BY COMPANY.	
	Deposit.	Sum.	Premium.	Sum.
1, . . .	$428 57	$428 57	$142 86	$571 43
2, . . .	571 43	1000 00	–	–

Now there is no provision on any of these contracts for expenses, so if there are to be any, some provision must be made for them in addition to the net premium. And if the law is not absolute as to the number dying each year, but only approaches the assumption as the numbers are greatly multiplied, there must be some addition on that account, especially if legislation has stepped in and in effect forbidden any policy's reserve to be used to meet any claim but its own. How shall this addition be made?

Observe that the self-insurance fund is a pure matter of deposit, occasioning no risk to the company. Indeed the greater it is in relation to the policy the less is the company's risk. If it yields interest, as it always does in practice, then a small part of that interest will be sufficient to pay the expense of taking care of it as it would in any other bank. Hence there is no occasion to increase the provision for expenses on account of this part of the contract, nor for any apprehended excess of mortality, for there is no risk incurred by it on the part of the company.

It is only in regard to the insurance parts of these contracts that the respective net premiums, $400, $444.44 and $571.43, need to be increased at all. And why should they not be increased in proportion to the insurance to be done by the company under such contracts, that is, the insurance value of each? This is the practical question now before every life-insurance company in this country, and it is several times more important than any other, for other things depend on it. By the antiquated blunder of which I have spoken, not the slightest regard was paid to the insurance value of the contract in deciding the question of addition for expenses, or "loading," as it is called. Indeed the thing was wholly ignored, and either a fixed percentage of the net premium was added to itself or one arbitrarily graded, but always producing, most absurdly, the largest margin on the largest premium relative to a given amount of policy.

Under the hypothesis above, the insurance value of the first or whole-life policy is found thus: The value of the first risk of $800, is $200 in hand. There are three chances out of four of having the second risk of $600 to carry for $200 which is worth $150, and there are two chances out of four of having the third risk of $400 to carry for $200, which is worth $100. So that the insurance value of the first or whole-life policy is $450; of the three-year endowment, $296.30; of the two-year endowment, $142.86.

These insurance values at the start measure the interest of the respective policies in the company as an insurance company and the additions for insurance expenses and mortality contingency should plainly be in proportion to them. Suppose we need an addition or loading to the whole-life premium of $90. This is 20 per cent. of the insurance value, and equity demands simply that the same percentage of the insurance values of the other policies should be added to their net premiums, making them respectively $490, $503.70 and $600. But the old blunder starting with the same premium on the whole-life policy, and loading by a percentage of 22½ per cent. of itself to make it, would make the premiums $490, $544.44 and $700, thus giving the shortest endowment policy which has the least insurance by the company, besides its larger expense on its larger deposit, the butt end by $100 of the insurance expenses. Look at it thus, and ponder on it.

| | THE EQUITABLE THING. | | THE ANCIENT BLUNDER. | |
	Gross Premium.	Margin.	Gross Premium.	Margin.
Life, . . .	$490 00	$90 00	$490 00	$90 00
3-year Endow., .	503 70	59 26	544 44	100 00
2-year Endow., .	600 00	28 57	700 00	128 57

Here is the fountain of the present trouble with life insurance. It is not the excessiveness of the premiums, but the violation of equity in *loading* them. And even this would do no practical mischief, however theoretically absurd, if the companies did not proceed to assess insurance expenses, beginning with agents' commissions, *in the same way*, and then aggravate the iniquity, whenever an already overtaxed member seeks to withdraw, by basing the surrender charge as absurdly on the self-insurance instead of the insurance value. *This* it is that has brought matters to such a pass that an old actuary hardly dares to turn a street corner suddenly, lest he should meet an irate short-endowment victim who will break more than one-tenth of the decalogue over his head. The blunder once found out is almost as ridiculous as it would be to harness our horses tail foremost, and would go out of use as speedily, but for the sanction that has been given to it by long usage, and the cheek of that cheekiest of all apostles, the life-insurance agent.

If I have succeeded in establishing in the reader's mind the distinction between the self-insurance and the insurance done by the company, which takes place in widely and ever-varying proportions under every policy, he is now prepared to appreciate the actual figures of the case, to be astounded at Mr. Winston's attempted *coup d'etat* and still more at the libellous utterance of the Charter Oak against the proposed system of Savings Bank Life Insurance. I give below the present premiums of the Mutual Life for a policy of $1,000, payable at a given age or on previous death and the proposed premiums with their respective margins over, or additions to, the net premiums by the American Mortality at four per cent., and the savings-bank premiums, proposed by me for the same policies, with their margins over the Actuaries', at four cent., which are of course a little less than they would be, compared with the American Mortality.

Policy for $1,000, at the age of 40, payable at a Given Age or Previous Death.

AGE OF PAYMENT.	SAVINGS BANK.		MUTUAL LIFE.			
	Premium.	Margin.	Proposed		Present	
			Premium.	Margin.	Premium.	Margin.
50, . .	$89 97	$4 11	$94 00	$8 54	$106 90	$21 44
55, . .	59 21	4 44	59 60	5 42	69 49	15 31
60, . .	45 48	5 27	43 36	3 94	51 78	12 36
65, . .	38 65	6 31	34 50	3 14	42 10	10 74
70, . .	35 32	7 40	29 45	2 68	36 91	10 14
75, . .	34 01	8 51	26 66	2 42	33 68	9 44
96 or 100,	34 03*	10 35	24 58	2 23	31 30	8 95

The premium for the longest term under the Savings Bank system being larger, by thirty-three cents than the *present* Mutual Life premium for the same term, it is pretty evident that the Charter Oak is mistaken in saying that the companies—except one—have declined my plan because it has " so very little margin for expenses." If the present life rates are safe and have margin enough for expenses, without the aid of endowment-insurance policies, then the savings-bank rates prepared by me have margin enough, *if the commissions and expenses are assessed equitably*, and it is an essential feature of the system that they shall be. On the contrary, it will be perfectly evident, I trust, on inspection of the figures above, that Mr. Winston's proposed reduction, now so happily defeated, worked as it must have been on the old plan of assessing commissions and expenses *on premiums*, could not possibly succeed except at a considerable sacrifice by the old members, and supposing it could, still, inevitably, the long

---

* This is what a whole-life premium *would be* on the Savings Bank plan. In fact, it is not proposed to issue this absurd policy under it, but to stop at 75.

policies would unjustly burden the short ones—which is as much as to say that it could not possibly succeed unless the expenses can be reduced to little or nothing and the stock of fools be largely increased in the land.

ELIZUR WRIGHT.

BOSTON, December 18, 1872.

Chapter VI.

BLACK AND WHITE MAIL.

The effect on the free American press of some two hundred life-insurance companies, hungrily competing with each other in every considerable city and village of the thirty-seven States and twelve Territories, is a most interesting study. The multiplication of policy-holders is a necessity of the business. The dispersion of the risks over a wide extent of surface is a great advantage, tending to neutralize the effects of local epidemics. Hence every company seeks to recommend itself everywhere through the press, national and local. Its agents are, if possible, everywhere. They are nothing, if they do not advertise.

There are, doubtless, multitudes of conscientious editors, general and special, of greater or less ability, who aim to give the people trustworthy information on every subject which concerns them, without regard to advertising patronage. But if any one carefully surveys the field, early and late, in regard to life-insurance, he will find marvel-

lously little evidence of their existence. He will
probably find no subject whatever, of any social
importance, on which American journalism has
done itself so little credit. The utterances of the
press have been sufficiently abundant, but their
character has generally been unreliable, if not con-
temptible. In fact, the American press, in regard
to life insurance may be almost exhaustively
divided into the two classes of the black-mailers
and the white-mailers. The former needs no
description. The executive officers of the companies feel themselves at the mercy of certain
advertising organs of no use to them, and look at
them with as much dismay as Pharaoh did at the
multiplying plagues sent upon him. So far as
dishonestly conducted companies are concerned, the
black-mail press, though an unlovely, is doubtless
a sanitary institution. But it operates with quite
as much if not more success on companies of the
best intentions. This they owe entirely to the
mystery in which their proceedings are enveloped.
They find it cheaper to buy silence on things which
they hardly understand themselves than to explain
them to the public.

But the white-mailers, always lovely and sapo-
naceous, are more dangerous to the people. They
are watch-dogs that never bark at all till it is too
late. They do not procure advertisements by
threats. But they allure them by flatteries which

do a hundred times more mischief. In regard to such profitable advertisers as the life-insurance companies, particularly the most autocratic, the motto of the white-mail press is, *nil nisi bonum.* It is only when the companies publicly fall out with each other that the white-mail press ventures anything like criticism, and then it usually betrays more ignorance than conscience.

The relation of life insurance to the press is well illustrated by what happened in New York in December, 1872, when the Mutual Life Insurance Company of that city proposed to reduce its rates on all policies without regard to the fact that most of them were already too low, unless the company should sacrifice old and retiring members for the benefit of new ones. The announcement was made with a prodigious flourish of advertising trumpets and at enormous expense. It was well calculated to strike terror into the hearts of other companies that were not in a condition to saddle upon an immense body of old members, with an accumulation of $60,000,000, the expense of getting and maintaining new business with inadequate premiums. And it did it. These companies obtained the opinions of professional experts, and rushed into print. Of course at a large expense. The advertising war raged for a week or two. It rained golden manna on the press, from both sides. For the mighty autocracy which provoked the

7*

war was not to be put down by the opinions of two
or three humble experts, who could easily be black-
guarded within an inch of their lives.   During the
melee the leading New York papers delivered
themselves of opinions in a most unwonted and
oracular manner, taking sides, on the whole, with
the allied host which opposed the reduction of
premiums, but betraying an amusing unconscious-
ness of the question which lay at the bottom of the
controversy, as to *the rights of the policy-holder in
his own accumulation, or self-insurance.*

As the writer was somewhat mixed up in this
fight he had an opportunity to learn a certain fact,
which may serve as a key by which any one sufficiently curious may estimate pretty accurately its
cost to the companies concerned.   As one of the
experts whose opinion had been published by the
allied companies, he with the others was made the
subject of a libellous and rather scurrilous attack
emanating from the Mutual Life office, pretending
to be from " A POLICY-HOLDER "* of that company,
and undoubtedly *by its money* inserted in nearly all
the New York papers.   To this he offered, personally, through the New York "Evening Post"
the following reply.   A sub-editor of that journal
who was present in its office could not assure the
writer that it would be inserted as a matter of jus-

---

* Understood to be an officer of the company also.

tice, because the article to which it was a reply had probably been paid for, though it was not in the advertising columns. The writer observed that it seemed a queer rule to exact pay for a defence against a libellous attack because the publisher had made money by it, but requested that the reply should be published at any rate and the bill sent to him in Boston. It appeared in the "Evening Post" of December 13, 1872, in a mutilated condition, an important sentence being omitted, and a bill was rendered charging 61 dollars for the 61 lines it occupied. This was returned, saying that the bill would be cheerfully paid when the reply was printed correctly. With the utmost politeness, the "Post," in its issue of December 18, then repeated the publication as follows, and the voucher for the final settlement will be found in a foot-note,* charging for 122 lines inserted once instead of 61 twice.

[From the New York Evening Post, Dec. 18, 1872.]

ELIZUR WRIGHT ON INSURANCE RATES.

The following letter we printed in the "Evening Post" a few days ago with an important omission.

* Mr. ELIZUR WRIGHT, . . . *To The Evening Post, Dr.*

		Lines.	Times.	Rate.	Amount.
1872. Dec. 18,	To advertising Card,	122	1	$0 50	$61 00

Please remit. Received payment for Wm. C. Bryant & Co.,
THEO. S. WEEKS.

We now print it corrected in justice to Mr. Wright :—

To the Editors of the Evening Post :—A " Policy-holder " in your issue of December 11 is disturbed in his mind, or has a mind to disturb the public, because certain actuaries, of whom I am one, have disapproved the reduction of rates in the Mutual Life, having previously approved as low rates for *stock* companies. It is on this difference of opinion in the two different cases that he wants to know whether we are " consulting actuaries " or " consulting weathercocks." This is good as it stands. If "Policy-holder" has been in the Mutual Life long enough to be *insuring himself* about half the face of his policy—and, if he does not understand what this means, perhaps Professor Bartlett will explain it to him —and he wishes now to play stockholder *gratis* to new members paying only *stock* rates, God forbid that I should forbid. On the contrary, I admire his self-sacrifice.

But to back up his " weathercock " theory on me, specially, this " Policy-holder " resorts to a falsehood and gross garbling of my words. This is the way he puts it :—

" Elizur Wright, speaking of the advantages of low rates to the policy-holders, says :—
" ' It is marvellous how little it is considered that the more you pay in advance, the more you insure yourself ! the more you have to pay beyond your just share of the expenses.' "

The only place where I have used language resembling this is in a note at the bottom of page 366 of the reprint of "MASSACHUSETTS REPORTS ON LIFE INSURANCE, 1859—1865, WITH AN APPENDIX." * I was not there " speaking of the advantages of low rates," and what I did say was this :—

" It is marvellous how little it is considered that the more you pay in advance the more *you insure yourself.* And how

* A work now out of print, and the plates melted in the late fire.

the more you insure yourself in most companies, the more you have to pay beyond your just share of the expenses."

This was aimed not against high premiums in a Mutual company, for it had nothing to do with high or low rates, but a false assessment of the expenses prevailing in too many companies, whereby a smaller risk is made to bear a larger share of the expenses than a larger one. The note, as quoted by "Policy-holder," is not very pertinent to such an issue; as printed by me, in connection with the text, it is more so. It was certainly intended to inform ancient life and all short-term endowment policy-holders, that whatever might be their respective premiums, they were, in most companies, paying more in comparison with other members than their just share of the expenses. So patent will this be to any intelligent reader who examines the note *in connection with the text*, that he will bear me out in saying this. If "Policy-holder" does not make a public apology for this falsification, into which he *may* have fallen unwittingly, then he meant fraud—"while Truth was pulling on her boots."

ELIZUR WRIGHT.

BOSTON, December 12, 1872.

The abusive and wilfully* false article of the anonymous libeller occupied 190 lines in the "Post," and without doubt cost the Mutual Life Insurance Company, $190. It was inserted in a large number of other journals that have the reputation of being more mercenary and expensive than the "Post." Any one at all acquainted with the extent of that newspaper war, in which the real question at issue was sedulously kept out of view on both sides, will have no difficulty in believing that the companies disbursed more money on it than they

* No apology was made.

do on fifty average widows.   After all, the expenditure in resistance was of no earthly use, for it was
not the published opinions of the experts or of the
editors that did the business; but the fact that
some of the policy-holders of the Mutual had con-
sulted able lawyers and found that they could, and
decided that they would, put an injunction on the
company if the absurd and inequitable project was
persevered in.   The expensive care which the
foiled trustees of the Mutual took to keep from
the public the true cause of their defeat, by extensively advertising a humble request of the allied
companies that they would suspend their reduction
of premium for the present, and pretending con-
descendingly and courteously to grant it, would be a
very amusing illustration of the high-mightiness of
bell-wetherism, if it were not such shameless
trifling with sacred trusts on the one side, and
degrading sycophancy on the other.   The whole
thing shows that the press in regard to life insurance, for the most part occupies itself either as a
foul bird of prey, or a silly decoy-duck.   This is
not much to be wondered at, and it is not worth
while to spend a moment in deploring it.   Money
has the power, under certain circumstances, to
reward and punish.   As long as nobody knows
exactly whose it is, the will that wields it has its
own way with the white-mail press, as well as the
black.   And that other portion of the press which

is rigidly honest, and about as ignorant as honest, will take care to avoid libel suits by entire silence. But money is not omnipotent. Once solve the problem and discover the key which dispels the mystery as to what is whose, and apply a little hydraulic pressure, and not all the money of all the autocrats, whether trustors or trustees, can keep the American press silent. And it is not the argument, but a little money, that will do it. As a quart of water may be made to lift an ocean, so a very little money may be made to lift from the lips of the American press that ocean of life-insurance patronage which is now used to keep concealed from the public two or three demonstrable, and to some, profitable, blunders.

If anybody offers a prize, of say $100, for a new tract, or essay, or hymn, or method of destroying potato-bugs or the like, in a paragraph of moderate length, it will generally be copied gratuitously in about every newspaper, daily and weekly, from one end of the Union to the other. The writer, after having become convinced by the New York premium war, that the companies on both sides, with a single exception, were resolved to go on perpetuating the old blunders in every policy they issued, thought it his duty to try the hydraulic pressure of a little money. And this he did not by advertising, but by asking editors of his acquaintance to publish gratuitously the following card :—

A Prize of One Thousand Dollars.

Three questions have arisen in the practice of life insurance, of great interest to the public:—

1. How to ascertain the proper commissions to be paid to agents, if any are paid.

2. How to assess the office or working expenses, including commissions, on the members of mutual companies.

3. How to ascertain the equitable surrender value of a policy.

A new system, called, for want of a better name, "Savings-Bank Life Insurance," was presented by me to life-insurance companies and the public, about one year ago, which answers all these questions in a way radically different from that heretofore practised by any company.

The old system and the new cannot both be right. Compared with each other, on these three points, one of them is probably wholly wrong and indefensible, while the other is an approximation to the right thing.

If the new system accords with science and reason; if it is in the main and in principle just and equitable in regard to the points above named, then the old one violates equity in regard to every one of them, and on *some* of the policies issued falls little, if any, short of obtaining money by false pretences.

There is no problem of social science more worthy of thorough discussion than this.

In the interest of policy-holders, present and future, and to stimulate inquiry, always better late than never, into the possibility of improvement, I offer A PRIZE OF ONE THOUSAND DOLLARS, to the writer who will first demonstrate that the old method of answering either of the three questions above is more correct, reasonable and equitable than that given by the "Savings-Bank Insurance" system proposed by me. This prize will be paid to the writer who first, within one year from this date, presents his or her demonstration to me, in print, with the certificate either of Professor Benjamin Peirce, of the United States Coast Survey, or of Professor William H. C. Bartlett, Actuary of the Mutual Life Insurance Company of New York, that in his opinion such demonstration is conclusive. And, in that case, either or both of these gentlemen shall be duly compensated by me for the trouble either or both of them may have taken in the matter.

ELIZUR WRIGHT.

39 STATE STREET, BOSTON, Jan. 13, 1873.

Of course it was not to be expected that such a card could gain any considerable publicity. It was sufficient, however, that it got published by a number of personal friends as a personal favor. It infallibly reached everybody personally interested in maintaining the old, and to them, lucrative blunders. Hence it is really equivalent to a prize of at least $100,000. For people who want to use other people's money are always liberal of it, and there are more than one hundred of them who can easily add $1,000 each to this prize. If there is anybody in existence who can win it, they will be sure to find him and set him at work, if the foregoing card has not. If the prize is won and paid, that fact will be published fast enough. The object will be gained, for the public and the press will then inevitably discuss and decide whether it was *fairly* won. If it is not won by the 13th of January, 1874, the publication of this volume ensures that that fact will be published in about every newspaper in the English language. It will be decisive.

It will make it absolutely certain that the companies which thereafter adhere to the old errors and *refuse to stipulate a reasonable cash surrender value* will have no business whatever to do except with people who either wish to cheat others or be cheated themselves.

Chapter VII.

A WORD TO THE LIFE-INSURANCE AGENTS OF THE UNITED STATES.

[From the Insurance Times.]

GENTLEMEN :—As one of the orders of men whose business it is to persuade other men to provide properly for their future well-being and to do their whole duty, I believe you have on the whole labored as hard and succeeded as well and been as poorly paid as any other. At any rate, I am proud to have belonged to your order. But a clergyman may be proud of his cloth, without denying that there have been false prophets, bad priests, and scandalously mercenary bishops.

Life insurance, sweetening every night the sleep of millions of people with tired brains and troubled hearts, and saving from utter desolation and want thousands of bereaved families every year, is a fact which could not have existed but for the life-insurance agents. When the world has become so good and wise as not to need gospel preached to it, and every man is a moral law unto himself, then there will be no need of life-insurance agents—and not much sooner.

If good work will not do itself, it must *be* done by somebody. And whoever does it should be paid according to his work.

As the actuaries of the past have adjusted the premiums on the various kinds of life-insurance policies they have failed —and I am sorry to have to include myself in this failure—

to notice that they were creating two distinct kinds of business on each policy that should be paid for on entirely different principles. This failure to recognize the correct analysis, and the consequent allowance of the agent's compensation simply as a percentage of the premium, part of which is for one sort of business and part of which for an entirely different sort, has led to great injustice. The blunder, once discovered, cannot be adhered to, without ruining the business of the agents as well as of the companies.

It is the aim of " savings-bank life insurance " to correct this blunder. Whether it is to be successful or not, the public has yet to determine.

The only objection, theoretical or practical, which has yet been brought against savings-bank life insurance is, that under it the agents cannot receive so large a percentage of the premiums for their services. This is undeniably true of *some* of the policies, such as short-term endowments, while of *some* of the policies of long terms, they will perhaps receive a little larger percentage of the premium than they do now. The fact is, that while the commissions on the latter class of policies are higher than they used to be, and about high enough, those on the former are scandalously *too high.* They are *reactively* too high, and the agent must inevitably suffer from the reaction at last. The commissions given for obtaining policies cannot differ much from a fixed percentage of the *Insurance Values* of the policies obtained without producing intolerable difficulties in making the dividends, and pernicious dissatisfaction with any that can be made. If the commission *is a fixed* percentage of the insurance value, then it is necessarily a *variable* percentage of the premium, because for any given age and amount the largest premium has the smallest insurance value, and *vice versa.*

But supposing the agent does on the whole receive less, for a given amount of insurance, or premium, it by no means follows that savings-bank life insurance will not be more profitable to him. He will profit most by that which yields him the most money for the least labor, in the *long* if not the *short* run. If the agent gets so much out of the premium as to break the company, it is plain how that will cut short his profits. If he gets so much that the company cannot possibly keep its policy-holders satisfied, that will produce a similar effect, by making it more and more laborious to procure applications.

Experience in any business naturally makes it grow easier and more profitable. But there are not many honest agents, who have been long in the business, who will not tell you that it costs more to secure an application now than it used to. Among the reasons for this, one is that *some* of the policies are necessarily unsatisfactory to the party insured, while the agent is compensated and other expenses assessed by a fixed percentage on the premium. Suppose the agent gets no more in the aggregate than he is justly entitled to, it is still certain that some policies have paid him too much. And this will produce as bad an effect as if others had not paid him too little. But, in truth, there is no policy issued by the company which does not pay the agent as large a commission as can be justified; as large as can be for his own profit in the long run; quite as large, probably, as he himself would be willing to acknowledge to any applicant. By urging upon applicants those that pay larger and much too large commissions, instead of driving his business he will drive himself out of his field, just as too stunt a wedge flies from the log instead of splitting it.

Everybody knows that an agent must live by his business, and nobody objects to it, provided the rate of compensation is reasonable. The true test of what is reasonable is, *that it can be satisfactorily explained to all concerned.*

The obvious advantages of the savings-bank policy which make it easier to work are, that, without much enhancement of the premium in any case, and a diminution of it in many cases,—

1. It stipulates an absolute cash surrender value.

2. This fact and the constant diminution of the surrender charge secures the greatest persistence.

3. The more the party insures himself, the less to an appreciable extent, he pays *pro rata* for what the company insures him.

4. It makes his varying relations to the company intelligible, from the first year of his policy to the last.

5. The terms of going out are as plain as the terms for coming in, so that there can never be any dissatisfaction to make the agent's work more difficult.

The following schedule of premiums and commissions on a policy insuring $1,000 entered at 30, will show the agent where the trouble comes in under the present system. Policy payable at death or

	40	45	50	55	60	65	70
Premium, .	$105 65	$66 35	$47 45	$36 75	$30 25	$26 20	$23 75
1st Commiss.,	26 41	16 59	11 86	9 19	7 56	6 55	5 93
Renewal, .	5 28	3 32	2 37	1 84	1 51	1 31	1 18

Here is a difference between the premium for the longest and the shortest term of $81.90, and nothing can justify taking the latter at such an excess of premium but an excess of dividend. For, suppose the party is to die within ten years, clearly his insurance will have cost him less at the lower premium, and if he does not die the excess of $81.90 compounded even at 4 per cent., will amount to $1,022—or more than he would get on the high premium—besides which he would have a policy with a reserve of $107.91. Dividends *might* justify the high premium, nevertheless, but *the commissions paid to the agent*, not to speak of other expenses, make this mathematically impossible. It cannot become possible till the commissions are less and all other assessed expenses less

on the short-term policy than on the longer one—on the high
premium than on the low one. Till this matter can be set
right every short-term endowment is simply a bomb-shell,
liable to explode and blow up the agent if not the company.
The only safe and permanent business for the agent is one
on which the policy-holder will be satisfied when it is fully
explained, and that is one under which the highest premium
will pay him less per $1,000 of policy than the lowest one.

The law which requires the net value of every policy to be
held in reserve, in effect divides every policy into two series
of insurances,—one done by the company which begins large
and comes to zero in the last year of the term; the other done
by the party himself by his own deposits, which can never be
used for any claim but his own, which begins small and increases
till it equals the face of the policy the last year. When we keep
these two series of insurances distinct—the insurance done by
the company and the self-insurance—we shall see why it is
impossible to satisfy the short-term policy-holder when we
pay the same percentage of his premium for commission—no
matter what the premium may be—as of the premium for the
longer term. The deposit or self-insurance part of the premium for the shortest term above cited, is $77.08, and of the
longest, $10.98. Either has got to accumulate at 4 per cent.,
so that if it is depleted by much more than 2 per cent., there
is no chance of dividend from that source, to say nothing of
making good the reserve. So much for the self-insurance
part of the business.

The normal present value of all the insurance the company
is bound to do on the shortest policy is $36.67, and on the
longest, $154.05. Now, no matter what the provision for ex-
penses may be on the gross or actual premiums, the dividends
of surplus cannot be made just and satisfactory to the policy
that pays the highest premium, if apart from 2 or 2½ per
cent. on his deposit, he is charged for other expenses compared with the other policy more than in the ratio of $36.67

to $154.05. That is, he must not be made to pay quite one-fourth as much. The self-insurance part of the business in regard to the expense it will bear is like a savings bank. It will bear as much expense and no more. The insurance part of the business must bear all the rest of the expense, and if it is not assessed in proportion to the insurance value of the respective policies—if a policy with a smaller interest in the insurance done by the company is made to pay more than one that has a larger interest—there will be the same row among holders when they come to understand it, as there would be in a company of stockholders assessed without regard to the number of shares they hold. An assessment of working insurance expenses according to the insurance value of the policies is the *sine qua non* of equity in dividends, and if equitable dividends are not to come in to make matters right, the premiums for short-term endowments in most companies are very. largely too high.

The savings-bank policies proposed by me assume a compensation to agents so high that it is necessary to enhance the premiums of the longest terms, somewhat, in order to pay it. And with such premiums it is on the whole about as good as is now paid on such policies. On other policies, while it is as much as it well can be, it is far less than is now paid. For example, on a policy for $1,000 entered at 30 for the same terms as above,—

	30—Death or						
	40	**45**	**50**	**55**	**60**	**65**	**70**
Premium, .	$88 23	$56 75	$42 03	$34 06	$29 55	$27 04	$25 80
1st Commiss'n,	3 30	3 11	3 32	3 70	4 19	4 72	5 26
1st Renewal, .	2 57	1 98	1 81	1 80	1 89	2 03	2 18
2d " .	2 57	1 98	1 81	1 80	1 89	2 03	2 18
3d " .	2 57	1 98	1 81	1 80	1 89	2 03	2 18
4th " ..	2 57	1 98	1 81	1 80	1 89	2 03	2 18
5th " .	2 20	1 42	1 05	85	74	68	·65

This means that in addition to 2½ per cent. of the premium as a collection fee—which is the same on the deposit as on the insurance part of the premium—the agent receives 3 per cent. of the initial insurance value the first year, and 1 per cent. of the same for four succeeding years, after which the collection-fee is the only commission.

These charges will bear explanation to the policy-holder, and he cannot fail to see that it is for his interest to take the shortest policy of which he can afford the premium. By the old plan the self-insurance is made to increase the cost of the insurance; by the new one it is made to diminish it, and takes away all motive to dispense with that element, as the "coöperative" plan attempts to do.

It is not the agents but the actuaries that have occasion to complain of the savings-bank plan of insurance, for the moment the company adopts it fully, it leaves no work which an ordinary clerk cannot do. All the calculations requiring any actuarial skill having been made in advance, the clerks have only to enter the various values of the policies, at the commencement of each policy-year distinctly in the proper books, and the ascertainment of the company's condition at the end of any fiscal year, is a mere matter of footing, and comparing assets with liabilities; and actual losses with expected.

And if any surplus appears, a clerk will know how to divide as correctly and equitably—on the "contribution plan"—as any actuary in Christendom. The necessity of permanent life actuaries arises from the fact that the companies, making no analysis of premiums in advance, find at the end of every fiscal year, the two businesses of *insurance* and *self-insurance*, indistinguishably mixed up in their books, and it takes more than an ordinary clerk to disentangle them.

This is a considerable item of needless expense. But for want of faith that the work will be faithfully done by all the companies, the State steps in—or rather thirty or forty States step in—and compel all the companies to transcribe the data of all their policies annually for the State, or rather for thirty or forty States, to make as many separate valuations, to ascertain for the satisfaction of each of them, the ratio of assets to liabilities. And all this at the expense of the companies. Here is vastly more needless expense. For if the books were kept on the savings-bank plan any State could ascertain by a few hours' inspection in the office, whether the company's statement was reliable, as well as in any savings bank.

Thus could the companies well afford to pay their agents better, if that were desirable. It is the agents, after all, in my opinion, who have the deepest interest in having the correct system adopted.

ELIZUR WRIGHT.

JANUARY 20, 1873.

Chapter VIII.

A RECAPITULATION.

The card on page 160 was sent in manuscript simultaneously to a number of leading journals, and among others to the "New York Tribune." The editor not having room to insert it in his next issue, addressed the writer a polite note, assuring him that it was received and would be inserted soon. After some days, and it did not appear; the editor, on inquiry, gave as a reason for not inserting it, a journalistic rule, that it could not appear because it had already appeared in other journals. A private correspondence ensued between the writer and the editor in relation to this journalistic rule and its merits, which was highly amusing to at least one of the parties. It served, certainly, to disabuse the able editor of the idea that a trick had been attempted upon his columns, so that he went so far as to invite the writer to give the subject a thorough ventilation therein. This offer was accepted, and the article which follows was bravely published in the "Daily Tribune" Supplement for March 15, 1873, though not in the weekly issue. The "Tribune," though it did not pay for heating the poker, is certainly entitled to great credit for displaying it to the extent it did.

[From the Daily Tribune Supplement, March 15, 1873.]

RIGHTS AND WRONGS OF POLICY-HOLDERS.

To the Editor of the Tribune:—SIR,—The existence of life insurance in the country of its birth after more than a century of trial, and its remarkable prevalence in this country, are sufficient evidence of its vitality. Our country is specially proud of its success in this business; its buildings are the marvels of our cities; its accomplished work of endowing widows and orphans amounts already to more than twenty millions annually, with a fair prospect of increase. Yet there are some clouds about it. More than any other business, probably, it professes equity, and oftener violates it, and almost always with impunity. It has always been covered with what bears about the same relation to its essence as leprosy does to the human organism, which a very little careful consideration will show.

INSURABLE INTEREST.

Legitimate insurance of life is for the benefit of the person or persons to whom the death of the individual insured would otherwise cause a pecuniary loss. Its limit is an indemnification of such loss, and it has no business to go any further.

The law of Great Britain does not allow a policy to be issued on any life in favor of any person who has no "insurable interest" therein, or, in other words, nothing to lose pecuniarily by its decease. But it does allow, and our law does not forbid—and this is the fountain of half the trouble that has afflicted life insurance—the policy to continue in force after the insurable interest has ceased to exist. After an insured person has become too old to labor productively, it often happens that he becomes dependent for support upon the beneficiaries of his policy; so that, irrespective of the claim on the policy, his death would be a pecuniary gain to them. The insurable interest has not only ceased, but become reversed. Yet, strange to say, neither in law nor practice has any provision ever been made for the timely and equitable cancellation of the policy on this account. Thousands of policies have been, and continue to be, surrendered on this account; but the surrender has never been regulated on any rational or scientific principle. Thus a policy which was perfectly legitimate and exceedingly useful at its inception, may be continued until it degenerates into a sheer bet, or, what is worse, into a premium for murder! It was in view of this abuse of it, perhaps, that the old French law prohibited life insurance altogether.

Our companies seldom issue policies on lives over 65, and never on one over 75. It would be contrary to law in ordinary cases, because there would be no insurable interest. Hence the proper range for life insurance is mainly between the ages of 25 and 75, and policies should not run beyond the latter age. The evil of their covering the period of second childhood is little felt yet in this country on account of the recent origin of the business here. In the mother country it is something terrific.

THE NATURAL PREMIUM.

Apart from the expense of conducting the business the cost of insuring $1,000 for one year at a given age, will be as many dollars as there will be deaths in one year of 1,000 persons insuring that sum at that age. The average fact is that not so many as 10 will die out of 1,000 at 25 in one year, and nearer 100 out of the same number at 75, so that the premium to insure $1,000 one year must be more than 10 times as great at 75 as at 25, the lives being equally unexceptionable. Hence, if a company agrees to insure a person the same sum, from year to year, from 25 to 75, the annual premium must naturally increase from year to year in the same ratio that the vitality diminishes. And, as an average fact, this natural premium will be exhausted by the cost of the insurance at the end of every year, no reserve being left or needed. This is, on the face of it, a very simple and nice method of insurance, and at the West people have gone wild about it, having too much reason for their madness in the defects of the old system. But if the company engages to carry on such insurance for a long or indefinite term, irrespective of the health of the insured at the commencement of each succeeding year, on the receipt of the natural premium due to the age, the healthy subjects, discouraged by the increase of the premiums, and having nothing to forfeit by discontinuance, will drop out of the company and leave a disproportionate number of sick ones to be insured; so that the company must inevitably fail.

THE ARTIFICIAL OR LEVEL PREMIUM.

The contrivance by which this difficulty is obviated is the substitution for the series of natural increasing premiums of an equivalent constant or level one, regard being had to certain assumed rates of mortality and interest. This, of course, must be so much more than enough at first that the overplus, being held in reserve with its interest, will make up for all the deficiencies of the latter years of the term.

Two cases arise: First, of term insurance, when the company agrees to pay the indemnity if the insured pays the premium annually in advance, and dies within a specified term, but nothing if he survives it. Here a moderate reserve accumulates during the first part of the term, which is wholly exhausted during the latter part. But few persons, however long the term, wish to be left with nothing but a worthless expired policy at the end of it, so that term insurance, on any terms, is little sought for.

The second case is that where the company, in consideration of the level premium paid annually in advance, agrees to pay the full sum insured, whether the person dies during the term or survives it. This, so far as the company is con-. cerned, is just the same as if he were sure to die in the last year of the term, in which case the natural premium (in advance) for that year would be the face of the policy discounted for one year. This is called the endowment insurance policy. For this the equivalent level premium, for a short term, is far greater than for a term insurance of the same term, but for a very long term it is inconsiderably greater. What is called the "whole-life policy" is always calculated as an endowment insurance policy, payable at death or 100 (or, in New York, at 96). The net level annual premium at 25 to insure $1,000 payable at 100 or previous death, is $14.72, and for the same payable at 75 or previous death, it is only $15.36, a difference of 64 cents per annum! Here is reason enough why a "whole-life" policy should never be sought for by a young man. But it grieves one to say how carefully this reason has hitherto been concealed from young men.

The substitution of the constant or level premium for the natural increasing one has two very important effects, of which one is, that a reserve fund has to be created on every policy. This necessity has been mostly ignored on the other side of the water, and the consequence is that a certain Lord Westbury, in London, at this moment, has in his hands a moribund conglomeration of forty life-insurance corporations in the process of what is called liquidation. Some years ago, Mr. Gladstone was so much worried with this state of things that he institnted, for the benefit of people of slender means, Government life insurance to a limited amount, through the British Post-Office. This is, of course, exempt from failure, but the premiums being high, no surplus returning and no proper surrender value stipulated, the people do not hanker after it, and it is not much of a success. If American life insurance has any superiority over British as to stability, it is because the necessity of a prescribed reserve has been more fully recognized here, and has to some extent been enforced by law.

Another equally important effect which, till lately, has not been recognized anywhere, is that it necessarily analyzes the policy into two distinct kinds of insurance, one of which is done by the company, and the other may be denominated self-insurance. The latter will be first considered.

SELF-INSURANCE.

If the natural premium to insure $1,000 one year at a given age is $10, and instead of it for a certain term, with endowment, a level premium of $40 is substituted, of which say $32 must by deposit and interest be in reserve at the end of the first year, then the person paying this artificial premium of $40, compared with one paying the natural premium of $10, is insured by the company for only $968, for which he pays a little less than $10, viz.: $9.68, and insures himself $32, by depositing in trust with the company the rest of the $40, which by the prescribed interest becomes $32 at the end of the year, and will be used to make up the $968 to $1,000 if he dies, but can be used for no other death-claim, because it must remain with the company if he lives. Hence by the level premiums all endowment insurance policies (including whole life) necessarily resolve themselves into two series of yearly insurances. One, done by the company, commencing with the face of the policy less the reserve at the end of the first year, and diminishing to 0 in the last year. The other, done by the insured himself, beginning with the reserve at the end of the first year and increasing to the face of the policy in the last year.

INSURANCE VALUE.

Leaving entirely out of view the series of self-insurances, which is nothing but a savings-bank accumulation, with prescribed or virtually stipulated annual deposits at interest, and regarding only the decreasing series of annual insurances done by the company, it is easy to calculate on the assumed rates of mortality and interest, the exact sum which, paid in advance, will compensate the company for carrying this whole series of risks, or be equivalent to those portions of the level annual premium which will be normally from year to year devoted to this purpose, and this is the *insurance value* of the policy—a totally different thing from the " net value," or reserve, which might properly be called the *self-insurance value*. The self-insurance value, or reserve, at the end of any policy-year, is simply what the company's risk in that year lacks of the face of the policy.

Now, though in the terms and conditions of the policy there is no express mention or hint of all this, and though in conducting the business for a century or two up to the present decade nobody ever thought of calculating the insurance value of a policy under that or any other name, the mathematical existence and importance of it is none the less real. Indeed, of all the values that need to be known for the safe, intelligent, and equitable prosecution of the business there is none more important than this. Yet, though the proof of this has been before the life-insurance world for full three years, and no expert, in the British Institute of Actuaries or elsewhere, has called it in question, there is probably not a life-insurance president in Europe or America to-day who knows what is the aggregate insurance value of the policies in his company much better than does his unborn grandchild. .Ideas, no matter how useful, are always slow in taking possession of the human mind, but their invasion is, nevertheless, irresistible.

It is only by knowing the insurance value of all the policies, along with other things, that we can know the real strength of a company. Neither the number nor the amount of the policies, nor the magnitude of the reserve, nor of the premium income, nor all of. these together, can enable us to determine the strength of the company. All these things have their significance, and need to be known; but till we have another element we can only guess between two companies which is the stronger.

When two companies are to be compared in regard to the economy of their working expenses, comparing their respective ratios of expense to either total or premium receipts is about as idle as it would be to count the buttons on the clothing of their respective presidents. The only thing which approaches a true test of relative economy is the ratio of the expenses to the aggregate insurance value of the policies. This aggregate bears so little relation either to the amount of the policies, or the total, or the premium receipts, that the ratio of expenses to either of these can have no use, except, perhaps, in some case to place in the front rank for economy a company which does not belong there. The deception which has been practised upon policy-holders and the public, wittingly or unwittingly, by the ignorance or concealment of insurance value, is something which will greatly astound a near posterity, and it might better be discontinued before that posterity arrives.

SURRENDER CHARGE.

Keeping in mind that every policy comprises a series of insurances and a series of self-insurances, let us consider how the entire contract can be equitably cancelled prior to the expiration of its prescribed term, in case the insured desires it while the company does not. If the self-insurance part stood alone, disconnected with any other contract, plainly there would be no more reason for the company's refusing to surrender the whole of the deposits therein with their accumulated net interest, without charge, than there would be for an ordinary savings bank doing so. Hence, whatever charge may be necessary to compensate the company for cancelling a contract valuable to it, such charge can have no relation whatever to the self-insurance part of the contract. It is only by the cessation of the insurance part that the company can possibly lose anything, and its loss here will be in proportion to the insurance value of the policy at the time, that is, to the value of the insurance yet to be done by it. This brings us to the conclusion that the surrender charge must be such a percentage of the insurance value of the policy as will leave the company as strong after the surrender as it was before. What it needs to be as a *maximum*, it is unnecessary to inquire here. But suffice it to say, it will not require to be much more than the commission or brokerage which will procure a new policy of equal insurance value, say six or eight per cent. of the insurance value. And what is worthy of particular notice is, that inasmuch as the insurance value of a policy, when limited to an age not exceeding 75, does not increase, the proper surrender charge for a given policy is greater at the end of the first policy year than it can ever be afterward, no matter how much the reserve may increase. And when the policy is not limited, but extends over the whole life, the insurance value increases so little that the surrender charge increases inconsiderably. This is radically different from the customary surrender charge, which is a percentage —usually from 25 to 50 per cent.—of the self-insurance value, and of course increases rapidly with the age of the policy. The absurdity of this barking up the wrong tree for the surrender charge is patent enough when, as often happens, the charge becomes larger than the whole insurance value of the policy; which means that it costs a man more to withdraw his own self-insurance deposit than the whole value of the insurance to be done for him by the company, and from which he releases it by his departure! The common rule of surrender, in fact, makes entire shipwreck of equity, as any equity court in the world would have to decide, if a case should ever reach it.

The true cohesive force of a life-insurance company is the surrender charge. If this is based on the reserve which has no earthly relation to it except being a security for its payment, it must necessarily be too small in the early years of the policy, and monstrously too large in the advanced years. This exorbitant increase of the charge, which one seldom discovers till after he has taken his policy, often induces him to drop it early, whereas if it had been the largest at the end of the first year, he would have continued. Where the charge amounts, as it does in almost all the present "all-cash" companies, to a confiscation of a large part of the self-insurance value without the slightest regard to the insurance value, it is anything but a cohesive force. It is doubtless the cause of a large part of the premature discontinuance, which is now pulling down the companies very nearly as fast as extravagant commissions can build them up.

ASSESSMENT OF EXPENSES.

Before any member of a mutual life-insurance company can receive his share of surplus, he must actually or virtually have been assessed and paid his share of the working expenses. The mutuality implies that this share shall have been equitably assessed. So far as a member has money in trust with the company, it is plain that he should pay his share of the expense which this occasions it, in proportion to its amount. But the reserve fund cannot well cost the company more, except for collection, than would the deposits in a savings bank. Hence, after setting aside of the company's expenses the moderate sum which it costs to collect and manage the reserve—it can hardly be one per cent. of it after a year or two—the residue must be assessed upon the members without any reference to the self-insurance on the policies, and not in proportion to the premiums, which contain more or less self-insurance deposit. But it must be assessed on what measures the interest which each policy-holder has in the company, considered purely as an insurance company, and this is nothing else than the insurance value of the policy at the time. If there is any logical escape from this, and money will buy it, the companies, none of which ever yet assessed their expenses in this way, will be in full possession of it within less than a year from this time. But if there is not, they will then begin to change their practice, to the great satisfaction and relief of the more self-insuring of their policy-holders, who now pay the more toward the expenses the more they insure themselves, and the less the company insures them.

THE LOADING OF PREMIUMS.

" Loading " is the addition which is made to the " net premium," to provide for commissions and other working expenses, and for occasional excesses of mortuary loss; the " net premium " being exactly sufficient to meet the policy claims, if there should be no expenses, and no variation from the assumed rates of mortality and interest; or what amounts to the same thing, if the death-claims of each year should be exactly what they would have been if the expected number ' of deaths had happened on policies of the average amount. So far as this loading is to provide against occasional excess of loss from mortality, and there is not more than the ordinary variation of the amount insured on one life, it is plain enough that it should be proportioned to the present value of the insurance to be done by the company under the policy, that is, to the insurance value at the start. It should be proportioned to this rather than to anything else. And as it has been already shown that nearly the whole of the working expenses should be assessed on insurance value, it is plain enough that the provision for them should be proportioned also to the same value. And as when the policy does not extend beyond the age of 75, the insurance value does not increase but gradually decreases with the age of the policy, a percentage of the initial insurance value which is sufficient for the working expenses at first will become more than sufficient afterward, and leave more and more of the margin as a safeguard against excess of mortality, which not occurring in any year, it will be returned as surplus.

To illustrate the difference between the new plan and the old in regard to loading, let us take a case. By the Actuaries' rate of mortality, at 4 per cent., the net annual premium at 30 for a policy of $1,000, payable at 75 or previous death, is $17.85. Its insurance value is $171.21. Let us suppose that $6.85 added to the net premium would be a sufficient loading for this policy. This is 4 per cent. of its insurance value, and makes an actual premium of $24.70. But if the same policy is to be payable at 40 or previous death, its net annual premium is $84.53, and its insurance value is $36.67, 4 per cent. of which is $1.47, making the actual premium $86. The only objection which can well be made against this mode of loading, which leaves the expenses of the self-insurance part of the contract to be wholly defrayed out of the excess of the actual interest over the low assumed rate, is, that a life-insurance company is at some expense for the collection of deposits, while a savings bank is not. This would be obviated, if we provide for the expense of collecting these premiums, which cannot well exceed 2½ per cent., by adding 1-39th of itself to each of them, and they will then stand at $25.33 and $88.21 respectively. By the old plan, which oftener than otherwise loads every net premium by 25 per cent. of itself, they would stand at $22.31 and $105.66. Granting that the former provision is sufficiently loaded, the latter is overloaded by $18.11. But if the former ought to be loaded up to $25.33, as prudence would seem to dictate, the latter is still overloaded by $17.27, which means that the party insured by this policy will pay needlessly during its term, if he lives through it, $172.70, with the slightest prospect of getting any of it back, because, as has already been said, expenses, including commissions, are assessed with the same neglect of insurance value. This overloading, and corresponding over-taxing for expenses, of the more self-insuring policies, has brought needless millions into the exchequers of the life-insurance companies, from this naturally popular class of policies. But inasmuch as most of this superfluous money has gone either into useless expenses, or into the pockets of the agents, who have thus received the largest pay when they added the least to the strength of the company, to the destruction of the dividends they promised, a small thundercloud is arising which threatens to put a new face on things before we have clear sky again. A distinguished life-insurance president to whom this difficulty with the shorter term endowment policies was explained a few years ago, admitted the error, and that it was, in effect, cheating that class of policy-holders out of nearly the whole of the overloading, and then argued against a correction of the blunder, that many people rather liked to be cheated, and that if the life-insurance companies did not do it, somebody else would. It will take only publicity and a little time to test the soundness of this argument.

TRUE METHOD OF KEEPING THE BOOKS OF A LIFE-INSURANCE COMPANY.

If the premiums of every policy issued were properly analyzed into self-insurance deposit, normal cost of company's risk, and margin for expenses; if the various values, also, were pre-calculated for every year of the term, and all of these things were every year entered distinctly, each under its proper head, on receipt of the premium, a great part of the expense of what is called actuarial labor would be saved, since the books would then show by their footings, at the end of every year, the liability for reserve, as well as all other liabilities. There would then be no necessity or excuse for the multiplied and expensive State valuations, which bid fair to cost at last as much as the death-claims.

The present method of keeping the insurance, self-insurance, and marginal parts of the premium mixed up in the books, and then looking to some Sisyphus of an actuary to separate them at the end of every year, and ascertain the liability for self-insurance, and the relation of the actual to the expected loss, is very much as if the silver and gold paid into the United States Treasury should consist wholly of ingots composed of the two metals, mixed in ever-varying proportions, and should go on to the books in terms of avoirdupois, Mr. Boutwell having to employ a scientific expert, or a corps of them, every year, to ascertain the value of each metal on hand, by taking the specific gravity of each ingot and applying the proper formula. Is such bookkeeping creditable to the last half of the nineteenth century?

SURRENDER VALUE.

There is no more difficulty in pre-calculating a maximum surrender charge, and consequently a minimum surrender value, for every possible year of every desirable policy, than there is in pre-calculating the premium. In fact, that work is already done. No such value, however, is ordinarily stipulated in the policy, but it might be with perfect safety to the company, and it would be immensely to the advantage of every honest company to do it. This would secure at least three important objects: 1. It would give the policy a tangible money value, making it useful as a security for a loan to aid in maintaining it through a tight place, or for any other purpose. 2. It would make the officers, in some measure, like those of an ordinary savings bank, more immediately responsible to individual policy-holders, so that greater public confidence would be secured, and the necessity for, as well as the labor of, State supervision, would be reduced nearly to zero. Here is something for harassed life-insurance officials to think seriously of. 3. It would remove all possibility of complaint from the tongues of retiring members, and avoid the backwater caused by too many of them. Everything being fairly foretold to and foreknown by the policy-holder—being inscribed in plain figures on his policy itself, from the first year to the last of its term—he will have only himself to blame if he changes his mind and retires before he gets all the insurance he agreed to take and pay for. He cannot then, as now, bitterly say, " I was enticed in by seeing in the company's prospectus a paragraph promising to give me an ' equitable surrender value ' in case I should at any time wish to discontinue ; but when at last I was obliged to do it, the company refused to give me anything of the sort, because it was not stipulated in the policy."

Here is a very swampy spot in the business (and a very rich spot for some of the companies), and the apology for a surrender value, whether in cash, or, what the party scarcely ever wants, " paid-up " whole-life insurance, is simply ridiculous. When, two or three years ago, the Auditor of the State of Ohio took it into his head to ask all the life-insurance companies their rules about surrender value, the answers he got and published excited a broad guffaw, and were copied by an insurance journal under the head of " Facetiæ." But they have been no laughing matter to thousands of poor men who have lost from $50 to $500 beyond any righteous surrender charge.

DIVIDENDS ON THE CONTRIBUTION PLAN.

This plan of distributing the surplus of a mutual life-insurance company is *per se* founded on obvious equity, and theoretically it has carried the day. But it does not decide the previous question of the mode of assessing the expenses, and when prefaced by the false method above exposed, of assessing expenses in proportion to premiums, it becomes practically either a farce or an impossibility. This trouble was evaded in the company where the "contribution plan" was first practised, because the excessive surrender charges in that company (it being an "all-cash" company) were more than equal to the working expenses, so that that burden was thrown wholly on retiring members. But if the policies stipulate a righteous surrender value, the retiring members will leave nothing in the company which can properly be applied to defray the working expenses of the year in which they retire. What they do leave must either be held as additional reserve against the impairment of the average vitality, or it must be expended in the future years to repair that average by the procurement of new insurance value of higher vitality. Companies cannot expect much longer to throw the whole of their expenses on the retiring members. Most of them retire too early, and the old members are consulting equity lawyers about their rights under certain promises of the companies outside of the policies. Hence if the "contribution plan" is not to be thrown to the dogs, there seems a necessity of assessing expenses on insurance value. If this is done,' and the books are kept and policies written as above described, "contribution dividends" will work admirably, and be intelligible to everybody.

THE TRUE REMEDY.

It is in vain to look to legislatures to correct the errors of life insurance. Legislatures cannot impair the obligations of existing contracts. As to future policy-holders, unconscious of their own existence as such, they are not likely to appear in person, or by counsel, before any legislature. The insurance corporations themselves, if they appear, are not likely to ask the legislature to tie up in any way their hundreds of hands. They are more likely to ask just the reverse. There is a funny story about a life-insurance president who spent several thousands of the company's money at a State capital, and had the amount carried on its books to the dividend account, where, of course, it appeared creditably if not logically. The only hope of having business-like business in life insurance, lies in enlightening the public mind, through the press and the lecture-room, up to the point of making all applicants for insurance insist upon being dealt with intelligibly and reasonably, or not at all.

ELIZUR WRIGHT.

BOSTON, March 6, 1873.

Chapter IX.

PREMIUM NOTES, LIENS, DIVIDENDS AND TONTINE POLICIES.

It would be easy, for one possessing the gift, to write a highly comic chapter on the various schemes adopted by the companies to attract business and get ahead of each other. The States vied with each other in making these corporations, and in some they were hatched by general statute, like chickens in an oven. Of course they must live, at least long enough to die. Hence a struggle. We have seen how the business, a mixture of insurance and accumulation, in all possible and ever variable proportions, was as incomprehensible to

the simple customer as a marketman's sausages,
or a boarding-house keeper's hash. All the more
for this reason was it susceptible of no end of
tricks, dodges, variations, short cuts and mirages.
"Plans," figure-heads and prophecies were the main
dependence, and for a while they seemed to be
conducting every chicken of a company to wealth,
power and glory. What was paid for these inven-
tions, in some instances, is quite incredible except
on the hypothesis that the directors were vegetables
of uncommon verdure. More than once some cute
chap has prevailed on a board of directors to allow
him a lucrative commission on all the premiums received under a certain novel "plan," of no value
whatever either to the policy-holder or the company,
but a decided detriment to the simplicity of the accounts. One of them even had the tact to get such
a commission commuted into an annuity on his life,
worth not less than $15,000, on the supposition
that his days will not be shortened by the brilliancy
of his inventive faculties. Figure-heads, of course
mostly wooden, have cost all the way from $5,000
to $20,000 a year. One, somewhat damaged by
the late war, was obtained by a southern company,
as it is said, for $10,000 a year, probably the best
bargain of that sort that can be quoted. As a general fact these speculations have not paid. Board-
ers who would have been well satisfied with meat
and potatoes mixed in the standard dish, could they

have known what they were and in what proportions, have become disgusted with the arts of cook-
ery which made them believe in something else.
They have left and are leaving at such a rate as to
discourage the most enterprising landladies.

It was demonstrated long ago, both by figures
and facts, that if the premiums are not more than
sufficient, and the reserve is not calculated at a rate
of interest considerably below that which may be
expected, a life-insurance company, unless it has a
large capital to carry it over the fluctuations of
mortality, is a very unsure thing. The purely mutual
companies have no capital at all, and the mixed
ones but little. They can rely only on a full reserve at a low interest. In a bad year, when the
death-claims are larger than were expected, they
have two resources: 1. The excess of the margins
of the premiums of the year over the office expenses. 2. The excess of interest on their investments over the rate on which the reserve is calculated. In a well-established company this last
resource is a very effective one, and will provide
for nearly double the average claims. By the same
token, in average years, unless the expenses have
been scandalously extravagant, there will be a considerable surplus of income beyond what is necessary to meet the claims and maintain the reserve.

No one who has examined the foregoing tables
will have failed to perceive that the company,

whether it is to have a surplus to divide or not, can safely take a part of the premium in the note of the insured. All the cash it needs, on the *self-insurance* part of the contract, is what it will charge in case of surrender. It can take notes up to the surrender value at the end of any year. The insured must pay interest on these, at least as high as the rate at which the reserve increases. But who wants to endow his orphans or himself with his own notes? Who can suppose it profitable to borrow money to deposit in a savings bank, especially if he pays more interest for it than the said bank returns? If a man can accumulate somewhere else faster than in the life-insurance company's savings bank, it may be wise for him to pay premium notes and use the life-insurance company only for insurance. But this is not the usual case. The premium would seldom be paid to any extent by note, and never on short-term endowments, if the party was not made to believe that the dividends of surplus would cancel the notes, and thus leave the insurance or endowment at its full face. To establish anything like a probability of all the notes being cancelled, if the policy should survive its term, they must be far smaller than the rule in any note-company, and should not be taken at all ou the first year of the policy. That 50, 40 or even 30 per cent. notes would be entirely or nearly cancelled by dividends was always a lie, wherever it was asserted. A company taking all its premiums in cash and refusing to pay an equitable surrender value, thus getting its expenses and perhaps more out of its retiring members, could undoubtedly make a dividend sufficient to extinguish 30 or perhaps 40 per cent. notes, *if they existed in it*. But if they did exist in it, as a general rule, the retiring members would not have been deprived of their money for the benefit of the persisting ones. In fact, the reverse would have been the case with those who retired early. They would have got their insurance too cheap.

What is true enough about premium notes is that, unless the expenses are much too high, the premium notes usually taken may be so much reduced as to be after the first year or two within the reserve, so as to be the safest asset the company can have. This, however, has been abundantly denied by the agents of the all-cash companies, who never tire of asserting the entire hollowness and rottenness of companies whose premium-note assets approached the aggregate equitable surrender value of their policies. To a cynical mind it would be an interesting inquiry whether or not the lies told against the stability of the note companies exceed in number those told about the dividends cancelling the notes. They must number by millions on both sides. If the author of lies cannot be bound for a thousand years, the next best thing is to simplify the business so that lying will have no reward except what it can get in another world.

It is hardly necessary to speak of that variety of premium note called a " lien." In this case the first premium is much larger than any succeeding one, and the excess over the level premiums that succeed, is a note, payable only as an offset or *lien* on the claim. It diminishes the insurance just so much, that is, in regard to the face of the policy, it is so much self-insurance. But holding the company bound for the face policy, the lien must of course be admitted as an asset. And as it is two or three times the net value of the policy, considered as an ordinary level premium policy, if the Superintendent or Commissioner of Insurance will be good enough to admit it as an asset, and at the same time value the company's liability on the policy as if it had received only the level net annual premium, the company may have spent the whole of the cash received on that policy and another, and still appear to have a full reserve. Supposing that the gross valuation, or discounting future margins into assets, by which the British life insurance companies have made their descent to Avernus so facile, is a valuable thing, any board of directors bent upon visiting that shady place, might afford to pay *something* for this little bit of the same sort of stuff. The invention is ingenious, but its sole utility in this country is to circumvent the State

Cerberuses. Companies that wish to do nothing of the sort, have thrown it aside, if they ever adopted it.

The various modes of applying dividend, or getting rid of surplus in mutual companies have already been noticed, pages 18 and 19. At the period there referred to, shares of surplus were assigned in proportion to premiums paid, without regard to the reserve on the policy. Two policies paying the same premium would receive the same dividend, and it might be fifty per cent., but payable four or five years after, should the policy be then in force. Yet it might happen that one of these policies had by its larger reserve produced twice as much surplus as the other. As the companies grew older, and a large surplus arose from the excess of the actual over the normal interest of the reserve, the percentage dividend became almost comically inequitable, though too serious for a joke to the early members, or holders of policies with small premiums and large reserves.

To Mr. Sheppard Homans, Actuary of the Mutual Life Insurance Company of New York, and Mr. D. P. Fackler, his assistant, belongs the honor of devising an equitable mode of dividing surplus, which they called the "Contribution Plan," because it simply returns to each policy-holder what his own policy has contributed to produce the surplus, either from over-payment on the insurance part of the contract or extra interest on the self-insurance part. This plan was adopted by the Mutual Life without delay, and the results were very satisfactory to the policy-holders, the more so that the expenses had been defrayed by the surrender charges on retiring members and the forfeiture of lapsed policies. It soon attracted great attention and discussion. Hon. John E. Sanford, Insurance Commissioner of Massachusetts in 1867, addressed a circular to a large number of actuaries and mathematical men, soliciting their opinions as to the best mode of distributing surplus in a Mutual Life Insurance Company. The replies which he received were published in full in his Thirteenth Annual Report, and are very various, but a large number of them approve substantially of the contribution plan. Prof. William H. C. Bartlett, of West Point, in his reply, uses the following very decisive language. "I find that this question has been solved by Mr. Sheppard Homans, Actuary of the Mutual Life Insurance Company of New York, in a way which leaves nothing to be desired. His solution is simple, direct and accurate, and I commend it to your considerate attention." After suggesting some verbal criticisms, he proceeds : "Mr. Homans' solution of this most important problem, returns to each member of his company not only what he may have overpaid, but also what the overpayments may have earned while in the possession of the company and under its control. He gives back the '*talents*' committed to the custody of the company, with their legitimate gains; and thus, iu my opinion, repairs, in the only way they can be repaired, the wrongs constantly but unavoidably committed upon individual interests, in the endeavors to keep upon the safe side of the contingencies inseparable from the business of life assurance." This was dated March 8, 1868. It was just as easy theu as afterwards to see that Mr. Homans' formula took no cognizance of the fact that the year of the policy from one payment of premium to another seldom coincides with the fiscal year of the company, aud that his expression for the actual cost of the year's insurance was rather vague, requiring a special interpretation to make it give correct results. But there is no use in putting *too* fine a point upon anything. In a company as large and well established as the Mutual Life then was, there was no appreciable chance of any harm coming to it from assuming, as Mr. Homans' formula does, that all the policy-years are coincident with the fiscal year; or, in other words, that no part of the apparent surplus at the end of the fiscal year consists of unearned margins, *if the share of surplus thus determined is not paid till the next settlement of premium*, as was the fact in the Mutual Life. In a newer and smaller company, of course it would be better to apply the formula only

9

to the policy-years *ending* within the fiscal year, and
not return the resulting contributions of surplus
till the next settlement of premium or the next but
one.   But in such a company as the Mutual Life,
with so large an interest account, and so little
chance of fluctuation in the death-claims, if there
are two policies, A and B, alike in all respects except that A's policy-year was coincident with the
fiscal year, and B's only just began as the fiscal
year closed,—that is, A's premium is just due and
B's just paid,—you may assume almost infallibly,
that B *will* contribute to surplus by the time his
next premium becomes due, as much as A is found
to have contributed already. ˙ If this assumption
does not turn out strictly correct, on account of the
rate of contribution falling off in the next fiscal
year, the succeeding dividend will be smaller, and
taking one year with another all will be served
alike.

The propriety of this view has been so well tested
in the late experience of the Mutual Life, that that
experience is worth dwelling upon, though it may
involve some disagreeable personalities.   If principles and facts are to be discussed, the persons who
make themselves representatives of the principles
and responsible for the facts cannot always be left
unmentioned, if we would.

In 1869, Mr. Winston, president of the Mutual
Life, and Mr. Sheppard Homaus, the actuary, be-

came dissatisfied with each other, for reasons which the reader will be allowed by and by to gather for himself from their own statements. Mr. Winston then applied to Professors Bartlett and Church, of West Point, for a searching criticism of Mr. Homans' method of dividing surplus, and those gentlemen then discovered, what had been patent enough to every mathematician practically connected with the business, that his formula was applicable only on the assumptions above stated. They devised and constructed new and very elaborate formulas, on the principle of the "accumulation formula," covering the whole history of the policy from the start, and reconstructing it, whatever its date, into policy years coincident with the company's fiscal years. Such algebra is as easy as travelling by balloon. The only difficulty is, when you come down to the solid ground of the facts, it may take a great deal longer to establish a satisfactory connection with them than it did to make the journey. Mr. Winston then procured from the company's counsel a legal opinion that the company's charter required the dividend to be restricted to the surplus definitively developed at the end of each fiscal year. It could not proceed on any assumption as to the surplus to be expected in the unexpired fractions of policy years equalling that of the expired fractions included in the last fiscal year. This done, Mr. Homans was ordered to apply the formulas of

Professors Bartlett and Church to the policies outstanding on the 31st of December, 1869, so as to
divide the surplus actually and definitively then developed, since the last settlement of premiums, and
no more,—for the critics of Mr. Homans were of
opinion that each policy had received its full share
of surplus up to that time, *if not more.* Mr. Homans at once protested against this on various
grounds, among others that the formulas were so
complicated, and involved so many quantities not
tabulated, that the work of making the dividend
would consume many months, if not years. The
dispute between Mr. Homans and the West Point
professors, which had grown to be voluminous, was
then referred by the Mutual Life trustees to J. P.
Bradley, Esq., since Judge of the United States
Supreme Court, Professor Newton of Yale College,
and the writer, all of whom had had some practical
experience in making life-insurance dividends. The
referees had a very delicate duty before them. They
were unanimously of opinion that while the West
Point formulas were mathematically correct,*their
application must throw away a great deal of labor;
that the interpretation given to the charter by the
counsel did not secure any better equity of distribution, while the change it involved would entail a
present derangement and needless future expense.
They recommended, therefore, that the charter
should be changed as soon as possible, and in the

* Substantially so. They were not free from errors.

meantime, being bound by the opinion of counsel, they suggested the best formula they could—that of Mr. Homans slightly modified, and more fully interpreted—for finding the contribution to surplus of each outstanding policy for the fraction of a policy-year from its last anniversary up to December 31st, 1869, and also another complementary formula, in case the charter should not be altered, to be used at the next calculation of dividend to find the contribution to surplus from December 31st, 1869, of each policy up to its anniversary in 1870, the contribution from that anniversary up to December 31st, 1870, being to be found by the formula used for the previous fiscal year,—or rather eleven months, on account of the change of dividend day from February 1 to January 1. Mr. Homans, using the formula above referred to, ascertained the sum-total of the contributions to surplus up to December 31st, 1869, to be $1,091,900.28, while the whole apparent surplus, including "unearned margins" so called, was $2,239,387.39. This showed pretty clearly that the method of division he had previously pursued was not very dangerous. But as there was no question that under his former distributions each policy had received its full share of surplus up to its latest anniversary, under the decision of the referees—limited as it was practically and rigidly by the *opinion of counsel*,—the $1,091,-900.28 was all that could be divided on the 1st of

January, 1870, payable at the next settlement of
premium in each case. The balance of $1,147,-
489.11 did not contain any surplus from extraneous sources, such as profits of forfeiture, for
in that eleven months the company had not made
enough out of retiring members to quite pay expenses, and Mr. Homans assessed 45 per cent. on
the margins of the fractional policy years, counting
as surplus but 55 per. cent. Hence under the rule
established by the learned counsel, at the invoca-
tion of Mr. Winston, the propriety of which was
not submitted to the referees, not a dollar of this
$1,147,489.11 could be touched till the next divi-
dend day, January 1, 1871, came round. But as not
only Mr. Homans but the referees had expressed
the opinion that there was no hazard in dividing it
—payable with the next premium—Mr. Winston
concluded, in spite of his legal counsel, not to dis-
gust his policy-holders, after all, by the blunder of
so small a dividend, keeping on hand an unnecessary million for a year! So without asking either
Mr. Homans or any of the referees, or even Professor Bartlett or Church, *how* this $1,147,489.11,
or any part of it, should be divided, any one of
whom, if asked, would have prevented him from
making the most comical blunder in the annals of
finance, he and his committee voted that each contribution or share of dividend ascertained by Mr.
Homans, should be increased 80 per cent! This,

of course, made the whole dividend for the eleven
months $1,965,420.50. It was in vain that Mr.
Homans protested against the vote as absurd and
contrary to the decision of the referees under the
rule of counsel. He had nothing to do but to
assign the shares, according to the vote of the committee. And the resulting joke may be thus illustrated: A and B are two policies, alike in all
respects except that A had its anniversary February
1, 1869, and B, December 31, 1869. Suppose, as
might have been the exact fact, that A's contribution at the end of the latter day was $81.69, and
B's $0.24. The vote of Mr. Winston and his com-
mittee gave A a dividend payable February 1, 1870,
of $147.04, and B one of FORTY-THREE CENTS, pay-
able December 31, 1870. The faculty of putting
things wrong end foremost could not go much further than this. A policy dated the 15th of June
was the only one which would get what belonged to
it. Those that came after were all to be robbed
more and more to gladden the hearts of those having earlier dates. Probably this blunder has been
fully corrected, and though it must have cost somebody a good deal of worry to do it, the fun of it,
to say nothing of its lesson, is worth a good deal.
Poor plodding actuaries have a dull time of it, and
an occasional joke of this sort does them good. It
is almost needless to say that after this experience,
the Mutual Life has returned to the first simple sys-

tem of Mr. Homans, of rating annually the contributions of the entire current policy-years of outstanding policies however dated, by the experience of the fiscal year just concluded.

After thus having narrated as clearly as the nature of the case would admit, the facts of this remarkable escapade, it is due to the reader to furnish him the means of ascertaining its cause.

The "Spectator," of New York, of July, 1873, contains an article headed "PRESIDENT WINSTON INTERVIEWED," which cannot be supposed to have been published without his full consent. This is an extract :—

"What were the causes of Mr. (Actuary) Homans' retirement from the Mutual Life?

"In brief, unfaithfulness, incompetency, obstinacy, impracticability and insubordination, in my opinion, were the reasons why the board rid themselves of him.

"Is it true, as he charges, that when the dividend system was changed in 1869, $2,000,000 had to be appropriated to correct a mistake that you made, in spite of his protest?

"It is not. I do not know how I can better explain this matter than by reading you a letter I addressed to a committee of the board which was raised in the year 1870 to consider certain alleged improprieties on the part of Mr. Homans. I then wrote :—

"Inasmuch as Mr. Homans, in one of his letters to me (which I have handed over to you), refers to the present mode of dividing surplus, I think it well to remark that the original cause of all this trouble and discussion about the addition of eighty per cent. to the last dividends ascertained by Mr. Homans was a mistake which he made in reporting the amount of divisible surplus to the board last year. Under the former system of anniversary dividends running with the policy year, the margins were all earned before the dividends were paid. Hence in estimating surplus as of a given date, payment in the individual cases being postponed as above, no such reserve was necessary. But when it was found necessary to ascertain the surplus actually earned on past business upon a given day, and to divide that amount and that only, Mr. Homans probably forgot the unearned margins in premiums accruing from that day to the respective anniversaries of the policies, and failed to include, as he should have done, a reserve for these among the liabilities of the company on that day. Mr. Homans at that time either did not comprehend or was afraid to admit the nature of his mistake, and the committee, considering his official statement and most positive assurance that a surplus existed (all of which, to use Mr. Homans' own phraseology, might have been thrown into the dock and the company remain solvent), could not see why it was not divisible. Had Mr. Homans known, and frankly explained his mistake to the committee, a remedy would have been sought, and much of the trouble of the past year would have been avoided. But his first error was increased by a disingenuous attempt to cover it up; and the committee, unable to follow the tortuous windings of his elaborate attempts at mystification, were compelled to take that course which in their judgment the interests of the policy-holders imperatively demanded, leaving a rectification, if any should be necessary, to a future time. In his intercourse with the committee, Mr. Homans manifests neither candor nor capacity as an adviser, while his memory in matters affecting his personal or professional interests is strangely unreliable.

"In accordance with the avowed intention at the time, Mr. Homans' mistake was subsequently rectified, so that each policy-holder had equal and exact justice done him. No expense to the company was involved other than that of the extra labor incurred. For that expense the company has probably been fully compensated by the reduced cost of the actuary's department since Mr. Homans left."

After what has been said this needs no comment. It speaks for itself. The reply of Mr. Homans follows, quoted from the "New York Herald," of July 19, 1873 :—

"Had Mr. Winston given to his interviewer the *facts* instead of *his opinions*, and allowed the public to form their conclusions, no notice of the matter on my part would have been necessary. The facts are these :—

"In November, 1869, I was the auditor of the Mutual Life Company, and Mr. Winston the president. He brought to me for audit the official quarterly statement of receipts and payments, prepared under his direction by the bookkeeper, in such manner that, upon investigation, I detected the fact that certain items had been improperly withheld in the final payments of death-claims to the representatives of deceased policy-holders, the books of the company having been already prepared, under his order, with a view to deprive such parties of said amounts so due them. To audit this statement by certifying the same in the usual manner to be correct, would have been justifying him, and involving myself as an accomplice in the perpetration of an act of dishonesty to the policy-holders, and a direct violation of the charter of the company. I, therefore, declined auditing the statement, beyond certifying that the same ' was in accordance with the entries upon the books of the company.' This certificate he passionately and violently erased, with the threat that if I did not audit the statement in the usual manner, he would find somebody else for actuary who would.

"That in this matter I was *unfaithful* to Mr. Winston in his scheme for defrauding the beneficiaries under certain policies of the company I admit, but *unfaithful* to the company, never. That to Mr. Winston I was in this matter *impracticable*, *insubordinate*, and *obstinate* is certainly true.

"Upon this occurrence, it of course became necessary that I should be *got rid of*; but 'Mr. Winston does little justice to his position in the company by stating that the *trustees* determined to get rid of me. If the trustees had come to such a determination, it would have been practically of but little moment, unless Mr. Winston so willed it. I was *got rid of* by Mr. Winston. Ever since he ousted Mr. Collins from the presidency by the secret collection of proxies, Mr. Winston has held absolute control of the company by keeping in his possession proxies of such policy-holders as, having given them originally upon the solicitation of his agents, have been too indifferent or too indolent to cancel them. Each of his trustees holds his place by the appointment or toleration of Mr. Winston, and from time to time, the most respectable merchants, who have been members of his board, have been *got rid of* for exhibiting *obstinacy*, *impracticability* and *insubordination*, amounting to *unfaithfulness* to Mr. Winston, in regard to such schemes and practices of his as he may not have been able to conceal from the knowledge of the trustees.

"His charge of *incompetency*, in that I was accountable for the fearful blunder in distribution of surplus in 1870, and that said blunder was occasioned by a mistake of mine, is simply untrue. It was occasioned by the direct interference of Mr. Winston, in opposition to the decision of distinguished referees, which had been approved, adopted and ordered to be carried out by the board of trustees, and he is responsible for the blunder, as he well knows. Mr. Winston never would have made this charge against me except under the excitement of feeling growing out of a circumstance beyond my control—viz., that I lately gave testimony, under the compulsory process of subpœna, before the assembly committee, during an investigation which resulted in his conviction of malfeasance in office, of the unwarranted use of trust funds by him, and fraudulent attempts at concealment of his conduct by false and altered entries in the books of the company."

One of the most remarkable features of life insurance at present is covered by the not very appropriate phrase of "tontine policies." It is very hard to understand why states that maintain laws against gambling, pure and simple, should allow the most pernicious sort of it to be attached to life insurance, and perhaps harder still to understand why State Insurance · Departments should maintain so mild a deportment towards a scheme got up on purpose to make their supervision a farce. Many of the best and soundest companies have abstained altogether from this seductive vice, and it deserves to be said to the credit of Mr. Winston that on the advice, as is understood, of Prof. Bartlett, his present actuary, the Mutual Life has discarded this enormity after commencing the practice of it. As long as the law allows such policies to be issued, it is a little dubious whether any demonstration of their nature and tendency does not do more hurt than good. The following essay published in the " Insurance Times " has been extensively used as a canvassing document by solicitors of tontine business. Nevertheless it is inserted here in the hope that it may stir up some public-spirited reader to ask the legislature either to suppress this sort of policy or repeal all statutes against gambling, so that those who *must* gamble will have no excuse for defiling a good institution with their constitutional and besetting vice.

THE TONTINE PLAN.

In every life-insurance company of large extent many policies are held by persons of considerable estate, who have no difficulty in paying the premiums, and who would by no means leave their families destitute if their claim should not be paid when due. Such policies doubtless contribute to the strength of the company, and it is no reason for refusing to insure a man that he is rich enough to do without it. A rich man may insure his house, why not his life? And especially if by so doing he strengthens an institution which provides an indispensable blessing for the man who has no estate but his life?

But if there were only rich men in the world, life-insurance companies would be little better than superfluous, a waste of labor. Their true function is to provide a substitute for wealth, an estate which a poor man can bequeath. They exist particularly for rub-and-go people, whose year-ends scarcely more than meet. Such people always compose a very large, if not the largest, part of the insured. This is so true that, notoriously, many of them *rub and don't go*. Insurance is a great blessing to them while they can keep it up, and they might keep it up longer if it did not cost too much.

Now, with a distinct view of these two sorts of people

who take life-insurance policies, we are prepared to define,
understand and appreciate the powerfully and expensively
advertised "Tontine Plan." It is a contrivance to facilitate
the going of the people who can go without rubbing, at the
expense of the *rub-and-go* people. Its sole and only function
is to make the richer part of the company richer *by making
the poorer part poorer*. It does not introduce into the
mechanism a single additional drop of lubricating oil, but it
takes from the wheels that have too little whatever they have,
and applies it to those that have no lack. It cunningly intro-
duces into the body of the policy a bet on the persistence of
certain annual payments, say for ten, fifteen, or twenty years,
should the party live so long. This little gambling arrangement, where the stake in the company's hands is the legal
reserve and the surplus, is, of course, a safe thing for it. It
holds a considerable sum of money for which nobody can
call it to account short of at least ten years. This is a *very*
comfortable thing for the company when it happens to be as
much as it can do to show the legal reserve under the high
pressure of present expenses. But it is rich, operates in a
palace that Midas might envy, and will no doubt have the
stakes ready to fork over at the end of a decade. Such is the
presumption. How about the parties to the little game,
by which is meant the tontine feature as distinct from the
insurance?

The losers are, first, those who have died in the meantime,
and, second, those who have lapsed or forfeited their policies. The winners are those who have survived and kept
their policies in force—supposing the company pays them
what the losers have lost, a supposition that calls for a certain
amount of faith. The losers who have died, have lost by the
tontine bet only such surplus as had accrued up to the time
of their death. This part of the loss,—much the smallest,
probably, for in ten years there are commonly many lapses
to one death, and surplus is always small compared with

reserve,—falls equally on rich and poor. So that the game—one loves to call it a *little* game—is fair enough, as a game, in regard to this part of it. The losers who have lapsed, have lost both surplus and reserve, as they existed at the date of lapse. This is what, without exactly knowing its amount, they bet on their ability to meet ten, fifteen or twenty annual payments. Here the bulk of the loss is sure to fall on those least able to bear it, and the winnings go to those who least need them. As a game of long purses against short ones, it can hardly be said to be fair. At any rate, the average effect must be exactly the reverse of the avowed object of the institution. It is as if a temperance society should endeavor to promote its cause by establishing a liquor saloon under its lecture room, or a church should support its minister by a lottery..

Insurance is necessarily, to a certain extent, a game of chance. Its peculiar benefit arises out of this fact. But the hazard should be kept at a *minimum*. The little appended game, called the "Tontine Plan," is wholly extraneous, superfluous and unnecessary. It could not possibly flourish if the fools were all dead, or nearly all. For that matter, we know that highly gullible but not unworthy people so abound, that lotteries and many other sorts of gambling could flourish, if only legislatures would give sufficient corporate facilities. Why they allow their creatures who are authorized to deal in life-insurance to entrap the unwary by these tontine plans, might perhaps become known to the public if the advertisements of them were not too profitable to admit of free discussion in the daily press.

Chapter X.

The Money Question in Relation to Life Insurance.

[From the Insurance Times.]

As concerned in contracts of the longest duration, a life-insurance company has a deeper interest in the constancy of the money unit than any other financial institution. The latest Massachusetts Report gives a list of fifty-five life-insurance companies of which the gross assets, using the existing money unit, are $290,563,953.47, while the present value of the future liabilities, using the same unit, are $261,662,482.40, showing a surplus as regards policy-holders, of $28,901,471.07. Now, on the assumption that the unit of this numerical statement is to remain a constant or fixed quantity in regard to value, or that its value will not vary materially in the process of time, this statement only needs to be true to be highly satisfactory to the policy-holders.

But unfortunately the value of this money unit, which has varied exceedingly in the last twelve years, is by no means fixed for the future, but is left at the mercy of causes which are sure to produce not only fluctuations, but such as are incapable of confinement within predicted limits. Compared with the sum which would appear by using the unit of the gold coinage, the least variable standard of value known among men, the gross assets of the above companies are now only about $254,900,000. As the gross liabilities, except to a very small extent, will not mature till a distant day, and *may* then have to be paid in a currency as valuable as gold, it is too plain that a slight cloud rests on the question of the average future solvency of these companies. For, if we are to have specie payment by and by, instead of there being a surplus now, as regards policy-holders, of nearly $29,000,000, there is really a present deficiency of about $6,000,000. On the contrary, if we are not to have specie payment by and by, but a fluctuating descent towards nothingness, of which no prophet can foretell the law of curvature, then, though the assets are at present abundant, no prudent man will be tempted to add to them, because the probability is that he will have paid more valuable dollars than his heirs will receive. The actuary, having made careful observations for a series of years, on the rates of interest and mortality, bases the business of life insurance on certain assumptions in regard to these two things which he regards as perfectly safe. Supposing them to be so, in vain are all his labors, unless the value of the money unit of his calculations is to be as constant, at the least, as that of a given weight of pure gold. If a legislature steps in and decrees that a piece of paper which is worth only x cents in the market, while a gold dollar is worth 100, shall be the dollar or money unit, and the life-insurance company reserves accordingly, carrying $1—x$ per cent. of its reserve to dividend, on account of this interference, the actuary may as well retire, and amuse himself, as he can, in the abstract wilderness of imaginary quantities. The legislative wisdom has simply made the assured solvency of a life-insurance company an insoluble problem.

The importance of this subject, in the present attitude of life insurance, is my excuse for venturing a few words on the elementary principles of money and the stability of its unit.

Money, as known to us, is the product, more or less entirely, of legislation; and consists, practically, either of metals coined by the government, or the promises of the government, or of individuals or corporations authorized by it, to pay such coins; or, theoretically, the expression of the sovereign will of the government that certain pieces of paper, without regard to any intrinsic value they have, shall be received and used as money.

We commonly call money the measure or standard of

value, and this, perhaps, is as far as we can go without considering the meaning of the word *value*. Value is not an inherent quality of any object, material or immaterial. Neither gold nor wheat has any value in itself. The value lies in the affection of the mind of the valuer towards the thing valued. This differs widely in different persons towards different objects, and this difference lays the foundation of that legitimate commerce in which the parties on either side make a profit. Value is either special or general, particular or average. When we talk of a standard of value we mean something which agrees with or represents the average attraction between a human mind and various objects. This standard is also called market price. If a gold dollar will buy a bushel of wheat, a yard of silk, or a pint of wine, we call the dollar the measure of the value of wheat, silk, or wine; but in reality the dollar no more measures the value of the wheat, silk, or wine, than either of them measures the value of the dollar. The only difference is that the dollar is used by everybody in exchange for almost everything, whereas anything else is used instead of it only in the rare cases of commerce called barter. The only reason why we select the gold and call it the measure or standard of the value of other commodities, is the convenience of bringing all other things to a comparison with the one which is the most portable and least perishable, and which, on account of the high affection of the average mind towards it, is most sure to bring in exchange for it anything which may be desired. Though value is not a quality of any object, it always depends upon the qualities of the object as well as upon the character and circumstances of the individual who values. Thus gold, by the qualities which make it clearly king of the metals, has been more universally, perhaps, than anything else, an object of desire and affection to human beings in all ages; and its scarcity, or rather the great amount of labor and search which is required to get possession honestly of a given quantity of it, has hitherto made it exceedingly convenient, when determined in quantity by coinage, as a medium of exchange. A starving man might be willing to give sixteen ounces of gold for a pound of beefsteak, and if all men were in a state of starvation, gold would be out of the question as currency. But, as things have been, no surer way of reducing to a *minimum* the fluctuations of value in the money unit has ever been devised than to fix, as that unit, a duly certified weight of pure gold. Yet almost the whole world has gone a long way beyond the use of actual gold as the circulating money. Promises of money have, in fact, become money. And inasmuch as these promises, when made or endorsed by governments do serve the purpose of money in the absence of performance, we have to consider a species of money which may be described as *the will of the government coined on paper.* This is the theoretical limit, to which the non-payment of promised dollars tends.

Let us then consider a purely arbitrary paper currency, made a legal tender exclusively for all debts, to see by what means any stability can be given to the value of its unit, or in other words how its purchasing power can be made constant or to approach constancy. Anything which is good to pay old debts, and which will be received in payment of taxes, will certainly have a commercial value or purchasing power in regard to commodities, and this will depend largely upon its scarcity. If by an irresistible government it should be substituted for an equal amount of metallic money, it would probably start with the same purchasing power. But not being convertible into coin, its future could have no relation whatever to the value of coin or the material of which it is composed. Naturally, if the government expenditure should exceed its income from taxation the volume of this currency would increase, and if the increase should exceed the increase of population and the demands of commerce it would depreciate in value. It could only rise in value by the taxes exceeding the expenditures, a hardly supposable case, unless the governmant should see fit to allow the people to regulate the volume by regarding it as a sort of debt (which is contrary to our hypothesis) to be funded at the option of the holder against the government. It is a favorite theory with some financiers that the perfection of paper currency would be to have it entirely independent of coin, and capable of drawing interest in kind from the government at a prescribed rate by being exchanged for coupon bonds at the option of the holder. They say whenever this currency should become excessive, tending to a rise of prices of commodities, then people would seek and obtain government bonds. Whenever it should become scarce, reducing prices, people would sell their bonds to the government to make it plentier and raise prices. Such an arrangement would unquestionably tend to steady the purchasing power of such a currency, but no such effect would be produced unless the government kept the price received for such bonds out of circulation by treating it as so much waste paper, and then it would be paying interest, and taxing the people to do so, in order to favor sellers at the expense of buyers—paying interest, in fact, on what could not be considered in any sense as debt without upsetting the logical basis of the whole system.

But the grand and insurmountable objection, in this country, to this coinage of the government's will into a commercial circulating medium, an objection which precludes any approach to constancy of value, is our popular government. There is no stable will to be coined. With an autocratic dynasty, it might be otherwise. At any rate we can imagine that in such a dynasty there might be a coinable will, descending from father to son, uninfluenced by the clamor of debtor and creditor classes against each other, deaf to expansionists and contractionists alike, and that it should so regulate the income and outgo from its exchequer of a commodity of its own creation, so costless to itself and so precious to the people, as to keep its purchasing power reasonably steady. This is barely conceivable. But when we have conceived of it we have conceived of something which does not exist anywhere in this age of the world, and still is no better, if it is not worse, than what nature has done for us in her rare and well concealed deposits of gold.

For the people who periodically create our government by a process which very imperfectly represents their collective or average will, much less their interests, to allow *it* to create money out of nothing, is simply allowing it to set up a rubber balloon between two factions of "bulls" and "bears," one blowing into it for expansion, the other sucking out for its collapse. Taking it pure and simple, it is clearly a project to be let alone. In the first place there could be no calculable stability under it. In the second, it would inevitably corrupt the government and lead to anarchy.

Now, we are suffering these very same results, the instability natural to such a system, enhanced by unproductive and parasitic speculators, under a currency professedly created out of the government debt, a debt which recognizes, in some sense, that constitutional standard of value of which the mint is the organ, *because the said debt is not duly honored.* In fact, all the evils which must necessarily result from a perfectly arbitrary paper currency, under any circumstances, will result from an inconvertible debt currency,—and probably more, on account of its being a patent, self-evident immorality on its face. It being a part of the business of any government to enforce the honest payment of private debts, its doing with its own debt what it would be dishonest for a private citizen to do with his, can hardly fail to have a bad moral, as well as financial effect.

I have referred to the moral aspect of the matter, because it more or less concerns the remedy for an evil, which, to life insurance, is simply intolerable. If there were no moral wrong, no unhingement of a nation's credit, in its open violation of its promise, the simplest and best way to arrive at stability of value in the money unit, would be to reduce the weight of the dollars at the mint to the value of the paper dollars to-day, and henceforward redeem the greenbacks on demand with these new dollars. This would remove the objection to immediate resumption, to which President Grant alluded in his inaugural of 1868, as the only one then existing, to wit, that of its injustice to the debtor class. If, however, such an act would be morally wrong, and would bring upon the nation discredit and disgrace, it must be avoided. But avoiding it for this reason, we necessarily admit that the suspense of payment is equally immoral, unless the government lacks the means, or the ability to borrow the means, to pay its non-interest-bearing notes on demand in full. It certainly cannot be said that the government of a country worth $30,000,000,000, and covering its full proportion of the gold mines of the world, at a time when the owners of gold are giving more than par for its six per cent. bonds, is *unable* to redeem every dollar of its non-interest-bearing debt as fast as it could be presented. Only the grossest ignorance or the most brazen impudence could make such an assertion.

We are brought then into the presence of a conflict of two evils. On the one hand, a perennial violation of the national promise; on the other, an alleged injustice to a not easily defined "debtor class." It is to be observed that the latter is temporary, that it is pretty exactly balanced, in a pecuniary sense, by an advantage conferred on a correlative creditor class, and that most people belong, more or less, to both classes at the same time. The case is very much like an inexorable, incurable toothache on one side, and the pain of extraction on the other. If the big patient prefers to endure the "hell o' a' diseases," rather than to have the dentist apply his forceps too suddenly, that artist will of course have the kindness to allow him a few months in which to screw up his courage. But the thing is not likely to stay in more than half a year, without throwing the balance of the ache largely on the side of the retained tooth.

I must beg the pardon of certain pedantic writers on currency for coming so near the close of what I have to say without noticing their argument, very popular with the parasitic class of gold gamblers, to prove that before the government can safely resume specie payments it must contract the paper currency to about the volume it had when the state banks issued it and redeemed it in gold. These writers, not happening to find laid down in the books they study, the fact that the volume of a paper currency resting on a specie basis depends not only upon the amount of commodities to be exchanged, and the complexity of the distribution, but upon the intensity of the public confidence in the solvency of the currency, have ignored it altogether. They should have studied the children's game with the paper torch, which, having quenched its flame without putting out its fire, they pass around a circle, each one saying as he holds it, "Robin's alive, as live as a bee, if he dies in my hand you may pack-saddle me." It passes till the last spark expires, and the more rapidly the sparks take their leave, the faster it circulates. So it is with paper money; the less the public confidence in it, the faster it will circulate, and the less of it it will therefore take to do a given amount of work. The people confide in the general government as being vastly more exempt from the danger of bankruptcy than any set of state banks that ever existed, and this accounts for the fact that they are contented to hold in their hands a much larger volume of the present paper, in proportion to the business they have to do with it, than they ever did of bank paper. Were it readily convertible into specie, and sure to maintain the same purchasing power as gold, they would be contented to hold rather more than less; in other words, the confidence in it being still more enhanced, it would circulate more sluggishly, requiring a greater volume rather than a less. But it

is useless to oppose facts to the theories of these writers, as
they are sure to fall back on their maxim, "So much the
worse for the facts if they differ from *our* scientific principles." One thing is quite certain, that if resumption has
to wait for the contraction these writers recommend, it will
never occur.

What resumption is really waiting for, is the waking up of
a majority of the people who are not engaged in gambling
under the name of trade, and not too deeply interested in the
privilege unwisely and unjustly conceded to the national banks,
to the very simple truth that every circulating note, as to the
difference between it and the capital which the issuer has to
hold idle for its redemption, is a loan from the holder to the
issuer without interest. They will then begin to see that as long
as the government is a debtor, it can furnish the best possible
currency, and ought to furnish the whole which is allowed to
circulate, by being a perfectly honest and honorable debtor,
paying its non-interest-bearing debt on demand, and borrowing at market interest all the funds necessary to enable it to
do so. It then gratifies every individual contractionist to his
heart's content by redeeming all the greenbacks he presents,
and every individual expansionist, by issuing greenbacks at
par for all the gold or government bonds he presents. They
will then begin to see that the national banks, in receiving
the full interest on the bonds which they pledge to the government to sustain their circulation, in spite of the tax under
the provisions of the National Banking Act, really get the
lion's share of the profit of that circulation, the whole of
which should belong to the government, or in other words to
the people. They will then see that if corporations or private citizens own government bonds, and are not contented
with the interest they get, but want to convert them into
money to lend at a higher interest, the best way for the government, if not for them, is that they sell the bonds out and
out to the government for greenbacks, and lend *them*. The

government thus saves nearly the interest, which is much more—in years, many millions—than any tax on circulation which it does or could get out of the banks, and the extra cost of hundreds of different editions of bills is saved, to say nothing of the simplification of the public accounts. A private Uncle Samuel who had a big money debt against real estate so ample and undoubted that his neighbors should be glad to use a third of it for money, in the shape of his I O U's, without interest, would not be likely to give away this advantage, or sell it for half its value, neither will a majority of our people, when they begin to see through their own affairs.

There is no sound policy for any life-insurance company, let the government do what it will, but to transact all its affairs in strict accordance with a specie basis, and exert what influence it can to arouse the people to see the necessity of it for their own interests as well.

10

APPENDIX.

THE ACTUARIES' RATE OF MORTALITY, WITH NATURAL PREMIUMS AT 4 PER CENT.,

Derived from the combined experience of seventeen English Companies.

AGE.	Living.	Dying.	Chances of dying in one year out of 1,000.	Natural Premium to insure $1,000 one year.
10,	100,000	676	6 76	$6 50
11,	99,324	674	6 79	6 53
12,	98,650	672	6 81	6 55
13,	97,978	671	6 85	6 59
14,	97,307	671	6 90	6 63
15,	96,636	671	6 94	6 68
16,	95,965	672	7 00	6 73
17,	95,293	673	7 06	6 79
18,	94,620	675	7 13	6 86
19,	93,945	677	7 21	6 93
20,	93,268	680	7 29	7 01
21,	92,588	683	7 38	7 09
22,	91,905	686	7 46	7 18
23,	91,219	690	7 56	7 27
24,	90,529	694	7 67	7 37
25,	89,835	698	7 77	7 47
26,	89,137	703	7 89	7 58
27,	88,434	708	8 01	7 70
28,	87,726	714	8 14	7 83
29,	87,012	720	8 28	7 96
30,	86,292	727	8 42	8 10
31,	85,565	734	8 58	8 25
32,	84,831	742	8 75	8 41
33,	84,089	750	8 92	8 58
34,	83,339	758	9 10	8 75
35,	82,581	767	9 29	8 93
36,	81,814	776	9 48	9 12
37,	81,038	785	9 69	9 31

The Actuaries' Rate of Mortality—Continued.

AGE.						Living.	Dying.	Chances of dying in one year out of 1,000.	Natural Premium to insure $1,000 one year.
38,	.	.	.	.	.	80,253	795	9 91	$9 53
39,	.	.	.	.	.	79,458	805	10 13	9 74
40,	.	.	.	.	.	78,653	815	10 36	9 96
41,	.	.	.	.	.	77,838	826	10 61	10 20
42,	.	.	.	.	.	77,012	839	10 89	10 48
43,	.	.	.	.	.	76,173	857	11 25	10 82
44,	.	.	.	.	.	75,316	881	11 70	11 25
45,	.	.	.	.	.	74,435	909	12 21	11 74
46,	.	.	.	.	.	73,526	944	12 84	12 35
47,	.	.	.	.	.	72,582	981	13 52	13 00
48,	.	.	.	.	.	71,601	1,021	14 26	13 71
49,	.	.	.	.	.	70,580	1,063	15 06	14 48
50,	.	.	.	.	.	69,517	1,108	15 94	15 33
51,	.	.	.	.	.	68,409	1,156	16 90	16 25
52,	.	.	.	.	.	67,253	1,207	17 95	17 26
53,	.	.	.	.	.	66,046	1,261	19 09	18 36
54,	.	.	.	.	.	64,785	1,316	20 31	19 53
55,	.	.	.	.	.	63,469	1,375	21 66	20 83
56,	.	.	.	.	.	62,094	1,436	23 13	22 24
57,	.	.	.	.	.	60,658	1,497	24 68	23 73
58,	.	.	.	.	.	59,161	1,561	26 39	25 37
59,	.	.	.	.	.	57,600	1,627	28 25	27 16
60,	.	.	.	.	.	55,973	1,698	30 34	29 17
61,	.	.	.	.	.	54,275	1,770	32 61	31 36
62,	.	.	.	.	.	52,505	1,844	35 12	33 77
63,	.	.	.	.	.	50,661	1,917	37 84	36 38
64,	.	.	.	.	.	48,744	1,990	40 83	39 26
65,	.	.	.	.	.	46,754	2,061	44 08	42 39
66,	.	.	.	.	.	44,693	2,128	47 61	45 78
67,	.	.	.	.	.	42,565	2,191	51 47	49 49
68,	.	.	.	.	.	40,374	2,246	55 63	53 49
69,	.	.	.	.	.	38,128	2,291	60 09	57 78
70,	.	.	.	.	.	35,837	2,327	64 93	62 44
71,	.	.	.	.	.	33,510	2,351	70 16	67 46
72,	.	.	.	.	.	31,159	2,362	75 80	72 89
73,	.	.	.	.	.	28,797	2,358	81 88	78 73
74,	.	.	.	.	.	26,439	2,339	88 47	85 07
75,	.	.	.	.	.	24,100	2,303	95 56	91 89
76,	.	.	.	.	.	21,797	2,249	103 18	99 21
77,	.	.	.	.	.	19,548	2,179	111 47	107 18
78,	.	.	.	.	.	17,369	2,092	120 44	115 81

*The Actuaries' Rate of Mortality—*Concluded.

AGE.	Living.	Dying.	Chances of dying in one year out of 1,000.	Natural Premium to insure $1,000 one year.
79, ...	15,277	1,987	130 06	$125 06
80, ...	13,290	1,866	140 41	135 01
81, ...	11,424	1,730	151 44	145 61
82, ...	9,694	1,582	163 19	156 92
83, ...	8,112	1,427	175 91	169 15
84, ...	6,685	1,268	189 68	182 38
85, ... -	5,417	1,111	205 10	197 21
86, ...	4,306	958	222 48	213 92
87, ...	3,348	811	242 23	232 92
88, ...	2,537	673	265 27	255 07
89, ...	1,864	545	292 38	281 14
90, ...	1,319	427	323 73	311 28
91, ...	892	322	360 99	347 10
92, ...	570	231	405 26	389 68
93, ...	339	155	457 23	439 64
94, ...	184	95	516 30	496 45
95, ...	89	52	584 27	561 80
96, ...	37	24	648 65	623 70
97, ...	13	9	692 31	665 68
98, ...	4	3	750 00	721 15
99, ...	1	1	1,000 00	961 54

The reader of the foregoing pages has not failed to perceive that the writer has been for some time engaged in a controversy, or struggle for reform, with the guardians of the people's money opposed to him. He has not, however, stood entirely alone. And he desires here to return his cordial thanks to the editors of the insurance press, who have almost without exception treated him with courtesy, and in many cases with solid support; in fact all they could, and live. His thanks are es-

pecially due to the plucky editor of the INSURANCE
TIMES, who has shirked no risk or expense in giving fair play to the most revolutionary utterances.
The volumes of that journal are invaluable, as con-
taining about all that has been or need be said, *on
both sides* of the disputed questions.

He also takes this occasion to thank his brethren
of the actuarial profession, whether agreeing entirely with him or not, all of whom have rendered
him important assistance, in a cause directly detri-
mental to their material interests, not excepting
Professor Bartlett, the present actuary of the Mutual Life. Indeed, to the writer, altogether the
most painful incident of this conflict is to be
obliged to say what he has of some of the life-insurance studies of his amiable friend, the West
Point Professor. His mathematical capacity nobody questions. But even a war-horse might not
know how to work a bark-mill till he had tried it.
One must first get the hang of any machine by a
little practice. The writer, at any rate, has made
too many mistakes himself not to look charitably on
those of others. Perhaps the stars can be got at
only through these asperities.

· To the young actuary, first of the Asbury and
now of the Northwestern Mutual Life Insurance
Company, of Milwaukee, Mr. EMORY McCLINTOCK,
not only thanks are due, but some proof of the able
manner in which he has won them. His bravery

in going, in spite of authority, wherever truth leads him, reminds one of the way in which his father, Rev. John McClintock, D. D., then a Professor in Dickinson College, Carlisle, Pa., in 1847, volunteered in defence of a hunted fugitive slave, and shared arrest along with his negro rescuers. Young Mr. McClintock's mathematical ability will not be questioned—certainly not by Professor Bartlett—and his ability to make mathematical logic intelligible to ordinary readers is such that the following extracts from his papers published in the "Insurance Times" of 1871 and 1872, inserted by his kind permission, will be fully worth the price of the volume.

[From the Second Paper, Insurance Times, October, 1871.]

The proper surrender value which a *proprietary company* should give, in the absence of any contract on the subject, is precisely the amount which it is to its interest to give. To determine this amount it must value the liability about to be cancelled by a rate of interest as high and a rate of mortality as low as there is reason to expect for the future, taking credit for future premiums in gross, diminished by a percentage representing cost of collection. To pay more than the amount determined by this rule would, except in the case of an impaired risk, be extravagant; to refuse to pay as much would be extortionate.

A *mutual company* should pay such sum, additional to the value just spoken of, as represents the withdrawable interest of the retiring member in the profits of the concern. If no rule be prescribed, whether by charter or by special contract, for ascertaining the value of this withdrawable interest, the determination of the sum to be paid is always and entirely under the control of the company.

The maximum surrender value is, as Mr. Wright has repeatedly pointed out, that amount which, together with the cost of replacing the risk in a satisfactory manner, represents the share of the company's assets pertaining to the policy in question. There can be no doubt, moreover, that the tendency of the business is to make the surrender value of policies as high as is consistent with safety. No one can pretend that a company is injured by the application of a rule by which the satisfactory replacement of the risk is secured. On the other hand, no one can claim that it is unjust to levy a surrender charge amply sufficient to accomplish this object; unless, indeed, a similar charge has been deducted already from the first dividend. This proceeding is sometimes resorted to, I believe, though (at least when premiums are taken in cash) without apparent necessity.

Exception to the foregoing definition of the maximum surrender value appears to be taken by Prof. McCay, in the current number of the "Spectator." He says:—

"The deterioration of life caused by the second selection, amounting as it does to ten or twelve per cent. among those who have been long insured, justifies a considerable surrender charge to those who withdraw in sound health and with unimpaired constitutions; and that no company can properly and justly neglect this and regulate its charge by the cost of supplying the place of the retiring member."

The article referred to is a very interesting one (leading, as far as it goes, to the conclusion that reserves should be based on Dr. Farr's table), but does not warrant the conclusion apparently reached in the sentence I have quoted. It is probable that Prof. McCay will not quarrel with me if I amend this sentence by adding the words, "by another of only average vitality." If the retiring member be *satisfactorily* replaced by a newly selected *risk of equal vitality*, the company cannot justly be said to "neglect this," or any other important requirement.

Where the surrender value of a policy has been fixed by previous contract, the company should, year by year, make the reserve large enough to cover (with the aid of such undivided surplus as may pertain to the policy) both surrender value and surrender charge.

The minimum surrender charge is, as Mr. Wright remarks, "not what the individual policy cost, but what it would cost to get another equally valuable." It must be determined by the company with reference to its *present* scale of expenditure, and in accordance with its *present* views of the comparative value of different classes of business. Even if the company pursue a stringent course, preferring to pay surrender values below the possible maximum, it is still important to it to know the limits within which safety lies. Hence, before a company can be said to have a correct view of the question of surrender value, it must previously have a correct view of the comparative value of different classes of new business— must, in short, have an intelligent mastery of the question of COMMISSIONS.

The scientific discussion of this question has been inaugurated by a well-known leader of opinion, foremost for the last twenty years in every important movement in American life insurance, Elizur Wright. His work in this respect is, as I believe, as important as any that he has accomplished. It may be expanded somewhat, perhaps, but it cannot be much improved.

[From the Insurance Times of December, 1871, and April and May, 1872.]

ON THE COMPARATIVE IMPORTANCE OF LIFE-INSURANCE POLICIES. (BY E. McCLINTOCK.)

Third Paper.

Some of Mr. Wright's views on this subject may be stated briefly, and I trust correctly, as follows:

1. Every life contract is composite in its nature, virtually comprising (1) an agreement to hold in deposit on interest a portion of the premiums received, and (2) an agreement to insure a varying amount, so calculated that each year the amount in deposit, and the sum really insured, or " amount at risk," are together equal to the sum nominally insured by the terms of the policy. This is the " Savings-Bank theory," so lucidly and effectively developed by Mr. Wright during his commissionership, and generally adopted by American actuaries as at once the most equitable and most convenient for the various purposes of a mutual society.

2. Of two insurance policies which are to continue only for the term of one year, that one is most valuable to the company for insurance purposes which yields the larger net premium. As the measure of comparative importance, the net premium on each policy of this kind is called its *insurance value.*

3. The *insurance value* of a policy which is to continue more than one year is made up of the net premium now due for the amount of insurance to be (really) enjoyed during the first year, *plus* the present value of the net premium which, one year hence, will pay for the insurance to be (really) enjoyed during the second year, *plus* the present value similarly computed in detail, of the (real) insurance for all further years of the term contemplated.

4. No scale of commissions can be intelligently adopted without due regard to *insurance values.*

These four propositions, each substantially originated by Mr. Wright, are sufficiently important and distinct to warrant detailed examination.

I.—SAVINGS-BANK THEORY.

Let us suppose that there are doing business in the same neighborhood, a life-insurance company, an annuity company, and a savings bank; that each allows four per cent. interest for money; that the two former make use of the Actuaries' table of mortality, and that the insurance company will not insure lives for a longer period than one year at a time. Let us also suppose that a man aged thirty-five, having some money in hand, wishes to apply it in the most advantageous manner to the purchase of two years' insurance of $10,000. What is he to do?

The terms of the insurance company are:—

To insure $1,000 for 1 year at age 35, ... $8.931
 "   "   "   "   36, ... 9.122

while the annuity company will, in consideration of $952.61 paid in at age thirty-five, pay back $1,000 if the party live to be thirty-six, and in the same proportion for smaller sums.

The second year's insurance, therefore, will cost our supposed applicant $91.22 one year hence. What he needs to do is so to invest his money as to secure $10,000 for his heirs in case he dies within the first year, and also to secure $91.22 one year hence in case he survives, with which to purchase the second year's insurance. He has his choice of two plans:—

He can secure the second year's premium by paying
  into the annuity company $91.22 × .95261, or . . $86 90
Which, together with the first year's insurance premium, ... 89 31
                                        ————
Makes a total outlay of $176 21

Or, he can put into the savings bank $87.71, which in one year will yield the sum of $91.22, sufficient to pay for the second year's insurance should he survive the first year. If he should not survive, it would go to his heirs. This being the case, he requires insurance during the first year, not for the full sum of $10,000, but for the difference between it and the amount to be paid by the savings bank, or $9,908.78, which insurance he applies for, paying $9,908.78✕.008931, or $88.50. Thus he pays out:—

To the savings bank, ...	$87 71
To the insurance company, ...	88 50
Total, ...	$176 21

Both plans, therefore, produce the same result—the two years' insurance costs him, at age 35, $176.21, which amount he considers, in either case, as his insurance premium.

So also, by making the proper calculations, he could so arrange his payments as to secure the benefits which are conferred by the "5-year endowment policy" in actual practice. Thus, taking first the supposition that he works through the annuity company, his accounts would stand, year by year, as follows:—

YEAR.	A Successive Endowments Wanted.	B Premium per $1,000.	C Deposit Required.
1, ...	$1,811 52	$95.2607	$1,725 66
2, ...	3,711 91	95.2418	3,535 29
3, ...	5,706 37	95.2224	5,433 74
4, ...	7,800 41	95.2013	7,426 09
5, ...	10,000 00	95.1797	9,517 97

That is, to secure $10,000 at the end of the fifth year the company would, according to its regular terms, require $9,517.97 to be placed in deposit at the beginning of that year; to secure $7,800.41 at the end of the fourth year would need $7,426.09 at the beginning, etc. Let us see where the money comes from:—

YEAR.	C	A	D
	Deposit Required.	Previous Endowment.	Cash Required.
1, ...	$1,725 66	–	$1,725 66
2, ...	3,535 29	$1,811 52	1,723 77
3, ...	5,433 74	3,711 91	1,721 83
4, ...	7,426 09	5,706 37	1,719 72
5, ...	9,517 97	7,800 41	1,717 56

The amounts in column A (corresponding to the reserve on an ordinary five-year endowment) are secured, therefore, by the yearly payments stated in column D. In addition to this transaction with the annuity company there is the insurance of $10,000 to be paid for, according to the regular yearly rates of the insurance company. Thus the total sums to be paid out would be :—

YEAR.	D	E	F
	Cost Endowment.	$10,000 Insurance.	Total Cost.
1, ...	$1,725 66	$89 31	$1,814 97
2, ...	1,723 77	91 20	1,814 97
3, ...	1,721 83	93 14	1,814 97
4, ...	1,719 72	95 25	1,814 97
5, ...	1,717 56	97 41	1,814 97

The foregoing statement represents the progress of an ordinary five-year endowment as analyzed into the two elements of *endowment* and *insurance*, in accordance with what may be called the "endowment theory," of life insurance. This theory is held more or less consistently by those who reject the "savings-bank theory." By the one theory the transactions of a life company are a combination, more or less complicated, of insurance business and endowment business; by the other, of insurance business and savings-bank deposit business. Let us now analyze the same policy on the "savings-bank theory." Our supposed applicant for insurance now deals through the savings bank instead of through the annuity company, as in the last case. The deposit account will stand as follows :—

First deposit, ...	$1,741 84
Interest 4 per cent., ...	69 68
End of first year, ...	$1,811 52
Second deposit, ...	1,757 62
	$3,569 14
Interest, ...	142 77
End of second year, ...	$3,711 91
Third deposit, ...	1,774 98
	$5,486 89
Interest, ...	219 48
End of third year, ...	$5,706 37
Fourth deposit, ...	1,794 02
	$7,500 39
Interest, ...	300 02
End of fourth year, ...	$7,800 41
Fifth deposit, ...	1,814 97
	$9,615 38
Interest, ...	384 62
End of fifth year, ...	$10,000 00

So that in case our depositor lives five years, he receives his $10,000 from the savings bank. In case he dies in the meantime, the accumulations go to the heirs; and all that he needs to insure his life for is the difference each year between these sums and $10,000. Thus:—

YEAR.	A Accumulation.	G Insurance Required.	E Cost per $1,000.	H Insurance Cost.
1, ...	$1,811 52	$8,188 48	$8.931	$73 13
2, ...	3,711 91	6,288 09	9.120	57 35
3, ...	5,706 37	4,293 63	9.314	39 99
4, ...	7,800 41	2,199 59	9.525	20 95
5, ...	10,000 00	-	-	

The total payments will therefore be:—

YEAR.	I Savings Bank.	H Insurance Co.	F Total.
1, ...	$1,741 84	$73 13	$1,814 97
2, ...	1,757 62	57 35	1,814 97
3, ...	1,774 98	39 99	1,814 97
4, ...	1,794 02	20 95	1,814 97
5, ...	1,814 97	-	1,814 97

By dealing through the annuity company, the insurer would pay to that company each year the amount stated in column D, and also to the insurance company that in column E; total, $1,814.97 per annum. By dealing through the savings bank, he would each year deposit the amount stated in column I, and pay to the insurance company that in column H; total, $1,814.97 per annum. In either case the cost would be the same, and the benefits purchased the same; so that it may be considered a matter of entire indifference to the insurer whether he act on the "endowment theory," operating through the annuity company, or on the "savings-bank theory," through the savings bank.

Let us now suppose that the three companies are one and the same. The net premium for two years' insurance, at age 35, will still be $176.21, and the company can analyze it in either way, as it pleases. Thus the cashier receiving the premium may keep his books on the "endowment theory," and enter it thus:—

By premium to insure $10,000 for 1 year, . . .	$89 31
By premium to secure endowment of $91.22, . .	86 90
	$176 21

or on the "savings-bank theory," making the entry thus:—

By premium to insure $9,908.78, ...	$88 50
By deposit on interest, ...	87 71
	$176 21

Every possible kind of life-insurance policy might be analyzed like the two cases we have considered on both of the two theories, which are equally admissible in all calculations regarding premiums and reserves, giving always the same results. But when we leave these subjects to discuss the economical questions which continually come up, such as loading, division of surplus, surrender value, &c., we are compelled to make our choice between these two theories or run the risk of self-contradiction. Of the two, the "savings-bank theory" is more or less explicitly conceded by most American actuaries to be more convenient and accurate.

A rigid adherence to the savings-bank theory (viz., that a life-insurance company's business is compounded of insurance and deposit business) would lead us to discard "pure endowments," "children's endowments" and "annuities" from our rate books. It would, on the other hand, effect a good pur-

pose in banishing from our minds the unnecessary and even
hurtful notion that the *endowment assurance* policy is in all
respects equivalent to a combination of the *pure endowment*
and the *term assurance* policy. This notion still crops out in
all sorts of places, and is the fruitful source of many miscon-
ceptions. For example, in a recent discussion of the surren-
der-value question, the author adhered rigidly to the savings-bank method in treating of ordinary life and term
policies, but abandoned it when it came to endowments; so
that the surrender value of the so-called "insurance part" of
an endowment assurance policy would be determined in accordance with the principles of the "savings-bank theory,"
and that of the so-called "endowment part" of the same policy in accordance with those of the "endowment theory."
Again, a singular belief, based obviously on the same notion,
finds currency in some quarters, to the effect that the "endowment part" exactly balances the "insurance part" in
respect to risk. A company was once solemnly informed, I
am told, by its adviser, that for the cause just stated "no
profit is ever made on endowment assurance policies by reason of diminished mortality!" This singular belief must
certainly lie at the bottom of the practice of many officers,
who accept risks for endowment policies which would not be
taken on the whole-life or term plan. Thus a doubful risk
would by some be speedily accepted for a five-year endowment for $10,000 which would not be taken on either of the
other plans for $1,000, the idea apparently being that the
quality of the risk is somehow improved by swelling the proportionate size of the premium.* In other words, if a doubtful risk were proposed (see column G above) for simple insurance of $8,000 the first year, $6,000 the second, $4,000 the
third, and $2,000 the fourth, it would be instantly rejected;

* Which, for a given sum insured, only reduces the *quantity* of the
risk.   E. W

but the same risk accompanied by an agreement on the part of the applicant to make a large deposit in the company's bank is gladly accepted.

The delusion is, that this deposit "reduces the risk"; whereas the fact is, that it is simply and purely a bank deposit, *belonging for life or death to the depositor*, and having no more real connection with the insurance risk than a corresponding deposit in a bank across the street would have. The amounts risked by the company on a five-year endowment issued at 35 are stated above in column G; and they remain the same whether the applicant pays the large premiums of column F, on which the company congratulates itself as "reducing the risk," or the small premiums of column H. The *insurance risk* is unchanged by getting the large premium; the investment department of the company is burdened a little temporarily, and that is all.

It may, however, be objected, that on this policy the risk is really less than on a life or term policy for $10,000. This is true. The risk of the company on this policy is only about equal to that on a term policy for $4,000. But the question is, would you take that risk for $4,000 on a term policy? If you would, you are safe in accepting the risk for a $10,000 five-year endowment—and not otherwise.

I have, perhaps, said more than enough to explain my reasons for agreeing with what I have called Mr. Wright's First Proposition. The still wide prevalence of inexact views respecting the "savings-bank theory" must be my excuse.

To sum up: the "savings-bank theory" and the "endowment theory" are equally tenable, mathematically. Life insurance is made up of yearly insurances *plus* savings-bank deposits, or of yearly insurances *plus* yearly endowments. Of the two theories the former is the simpler, and is generally preferred.

If the reader holds the opinion that the savings-bank theory is incorrect and untenable—an opinion frequently expressed by insurance writers, mostly anonymous—he may as well read this article no further. Objecting to my premises he cannot feel interest in my conclusions. It is always a good exercise of mind, when you disagree with a writer, to determine to your own satisfaction the precise point at which you part company from him.

II.—INSURANCE VALUE OF YEARLY POLICIES.

What I have set down as Mr. Wright's Second Proposition is, that of two policies securing insurance for the term of a single year, that one is most valuable to the company which yields the larger net premium, and that the relative value of each policy is measured by the net premium, which in this connection is called the "insurance value." This proposition may be thus sub-divided :—

1. The insurance value of a one-year-term policy, the age being given, varies directly as the amount assured. That is, a policy for $10,000 is ten times as valuable to the company as one for $1,000. From the point of view of the secretary, cashier, and collecting agent it may, perhaps, be regarded as more than ten times as valuable ; or, in other words, it may be thought that one policy of $10,000 is less troublesome and therefore more desirable than ten policies of $1,000. This feeling formerly found expression in the *policy-fee*, a tax on small policies. From the mortuary point of view, however, it is sometimes argued that ten policies of $1,000 each are better worth having than one policy of $10,000 ; and in view of the almost universal discontinuance of the policy-fee system, it may be considered as agreed that, on the whole, the company may justly regard all sizes of policy with equal favor.

2. The insurance value of a one-year term policy, the amount being given, varies directly as the rate of mortality indicated by the age of the party. That is, if a man at 40 pays (net) $10 for a year's insurance of $1,000, and one at 54

pays $20 for the same benefit, the latter policy is twice as.
important as the former—is, in fact, worth as much to the
company as two policies like the former. This view is in
accordance with the almost universal practice of the business
and the almost universal opinion of insurance officers. It
is, however, not *quite* so clearly settled as that twice two
make four. It is certain that, loading apart, a man aged 54
can afford to pay twice as much per $1,000 as one aged 40,
but it is not so clear that he should contribute proportionally
to the running expenses of the society. It is a possible
hypothesis that insurance of $1,000 is worth, morally, and
apart from the net payment necessary to cover the risk, as
much to the man aged 40 as to the one aged 54, or at any
rate more than half as much. It is, therefore, a debatable
question whether the loading on the premium for one year's
assurance should be a function of the premium or of the
amount assured, or of both.

Assuming the general opinion in favor of assessing expenses on such policies by a uniform percentage on premiums to be the correct one, it cannot be denied that a one-
year policy which contributes twice as much to the insurance
fund, and twice as much to the expense fund as another, is
worth twice as much to the company. Let it be observed,
moreover, that even supposing this now general opinion to
be discarded, the importance of estimating insurance values
on the general principles urged by Mr. Wright would not be
diminished, though the intricacy of the necessary calculations might be considerably increased.

III.—INSURANCE VALUE OF POLICIES IN GENERAL.

Assuming, therefore, the savings-bank theory as a basis,
and assuming that the net premium is the most convenient
measure of the value to the company of simple assurances
confined to a single year, let us now consider some of the
more complicated cases arising from the various combina-
tions of the elements of *insurance* and *deposit*.

. In a case already supposed, we found the net premium which a man aged 36 would need to pay for a year's assurance of $10,000, to be $91.22; and at age 35 for *two* years' insurance of the same amount, $176.21. On analyzing the latter premium we found it to consist of two parts:—

Premium to insure $9,908.78 for one year, . . .	$88	50
Deposit on interest, ...	87	71
	$176	21

The contract might, therefore, be described as a compound agreement, consisting of (1) an agreement to hold $87.71 on deposit for one year, at four per cent. interest, amounting at the end of the year to $91.22, and (2) an agreement to insure $9,908.78 for one year for an advance payment of $88.50, and also to insure $10,000 the second year for a payment one year hence (transferred from the deposit department) of $91.22. By this arrangement, in case of death the first year, the company pays over to the beneficiary the amount of deposit, $91.22, and the amount of insurance, $9,908.78, making $10,000; and in case of death the second year the whole amount of $10,000 is drawn from the insurance fund.

Considering first that portion of the contract which provides for assurance during the second year (age 36, amount $10,000, premium to be then paid $91.22), we may conclude that, one year hence, its value to the company may be measured by the net premium then payable, or $91.22. Taking next that portion of the contract which provides for immediate insurance of $9,908.78, we may measure its present value by the net premium now due, or $88.50. If, therefore, we add to $88.50 the present value of $91.22, we shall have the total value to the company of the insurance part of the contract, or what Mr. Wright calls the *insurance value* of the policy.

In finding the present value of business, which *will be*

worth $88.50 (or some peroentage of that sum taken as a measure) one year hence, we are not bound to follow the original standards of mortality and interest, but may use such assumptions as are warranted by our best judgment, having regard to the probable actual experience of the future, while retaining the original standards, of course, in all calculations of premiums and reserves. Mr. Wright considers it convenient to follow the assumptions—Actuaries' 4 per cent.— of his published tables. Pursuing this course, we should find the present value at age 35 of $91.22 at age 36 to be $86.90. Adding this, the present value of the insurance to be done by the company the second year, to $88.50, the value of the first year's insurance, we have $175.40 as the *insurance value* of the policy in question. And, disregarding the value, whatever it may be, of the " deposit part " of the contract, we may, by a like analysis, conclude with reference to any other policy, that its *insurance value* is equal to " the net premium now due for the amount of insurance to be (really) enjoyed during the first year, *plus* the present value of the net premium which, one year hence, will pay for the insurance to be (really) enjoyed during the second year, *plus* the present value, similarly computed in detail, of the (real) insurance for all further years of the term contemplated," a definition which I have taken the liberty to call Mr. Wright's Third Proposition.

The " deposit part" of a contract has its value, of course, even though a comparatively small one. We shall no doubt find, on investigation, that the best measure of the " deposit value" of a policy is, the amount agreed to be held in deposit the first year, *plus* the present value of that agreed to be held the second year, *plus*, &c.

IV.—COMMISSIONS.

" No scale of commissions can be intelligently adopted without due regard to insurance value." This remark, which

I have called Mr. Wright's Fourth Proposition, naturally follows from the preceding considerations. We may presume that a percentage of the insurance value of a policy, *plus* some other percentage of its deposit value, would best represent the pecuniary worth of the contract to the company. While not insisting on the expediency of a daily resort to calculations so intricate as are here indicated, I cannot but think that some knowledge of the results to which such calculations lead must prove of the highest value to those who may hereafter have occasion to deal with the question of commissions; and that the thanks of all concerned are eminently due to the Hon. Elizur Wright for the initiation and vigorous prosecution, in this connection, of a radical reform.